CIRCLES

Lessons I Learned While Rebuilding My Life

Melanie Harding

Circles of Rescue
© 2023 Melanie Harding

ISBN: 978-1-66789-387-7

Table of Contents

The following is a true story told to the best of my ability. Some of the names have been changed to protect the guilty.

Dedication

This book is dedicated to all the people who have fallen down and are looking for the strength to pick themselves up and move forward. Your courage is an inspiration to those around you. May God bless you as you grow and become the people you were meant to be.

Thank you to all of the angels who came into my life and gave me what I needed when I needed it the most. Your love and kindness will never be forgotten. I hope that I will follow in your footsteps and become a beacon of hope for others.

A few angels need to be singled out for special attention. The first of these is Dr. Pamela Walker. Pam started me on my journey and sponsored me to health. She reminded me that although I thought I was at the end of my journey, I had actually only completed 10 percent of it.

I would also like to thank Dr. Gary Cone. I was led to him during one of my darkest hours, when I needed someone to shine a light on my spirit and pull me out of the despair I had wandered into. As the years passed, he became more than my therapist. He has been my teacher, mentor, and friend, and I am grateful that he taught me how to grow and move beyond the life I was born into.

This dedication would not be complete without mentioning Jack Morgan Field. Jack was my boss and quickly became my friend. He showed me what unconditional love looks like, and I will be forever grateful for the spiritual, emotional, and financial gifts he gave me.

Words cannot express the love and gratitude I have for Pastor Nicholas Harris, a good and faithful servant who was called home during the COVID pandemic in 2020. For much of his career, Pastor Harris tended to his flock at First United Methodist Church in downtown Oklahoma City. After his retirement, he started Ariel Chapel in Norman, Oklahoma, where I was honored to have him teach me and help me grow spiritually. He introduced me to the ideas that became the Three Circles seen throughout this book. I am not the only one who is grateful for having known Pastor Harris. He shepherded many laypeople and ministers, and his absence leaves a hole in all of our hearts.

My final debt of gratitude goes to all of the people who came into my life and caused me harm, inadvertently or purposefully. The pain you gave me put me on the path to become the person God wants me to be, and I could not have grown without the scars that you left on my heart and in my spirit.

Special Thanks

I would like to give special thanks to Walter B. Jenkins. I hired Walter to help me ghostwrite this book, but he quickly became much more. He collaborated with me to expand ideas that needed to be developed, trimmed thoughts that should be used elsewhere, and organized my stories. He did this while keeping my story intact, preserving my thoughts, and staying true to my voice. His efforts have helped me share my story with the world.

My Private Island

Mom would have to believe my older sister and me if we told her what her new husband had done.

We waited for an afternoon when our stepfather was at work. We would have no chance if he hovered over us when we tried to explain to our mother what kind of person he was. When Mom was alone in her bedroom, we asked if we could talk to her, and the three of us sat on the edge of her bed.

I started first, confident that my sister would back me up. My sister had told me we were in this together, and that gave me the confidence I needed to set the truth free. I looked Mom in the eyes and didn't hold back any details. I told her how her husband had grabbed me by the throat and how I had to push him off while he tried to rape me. I told her how he had been preying on me from the time he moved in.

As I spoke, relief swept over me. Telling the truth set me free. I thought our nightmare was over and that Mom would stand up for us. I thought that she would throw him out of our house.

I was wrong.

My mother exploded with anger. She screamed and said I was trying to cause trouble between her and my stepfather. She defended him, saying he was taking pills called white crosses to stay awake while he was driving his truck, and they didn't mix well with his drinking. He didn't mean anything he did or said, she continued.

"Exactly," I thought. "He's a druggie and a drunk. Get him out of our home."

Then the other shoe dropped.

I looked at my sister and thought, "Okay, now you tell her what he did to you." We had rehearsed what we were going to say, and I waited for her to speak but the words never came. She didn't utter a single word. My sister had watched our mother yell at me and became scared, so frightened that she was not willing to protect me or herself. My sister had an advantage because in a few days she would be returning to Germany to be with her husband. That distance would create a safe space for her, a place far from the fear and dysfunction that had been the pillars of our home for years. In a short time, I would be alone with my mother and her crazy husband.

My sister's silence and my mother's anger left me alone on an island. There were no lifeguards, and no ships were racing to pull me to safety. I was only twelve years old and hoped the waves would not wash me out to sea.

I thought the truth would set me free, that by using my voice to stand up for myself I would be liberated. That wasn't the case. I had let the cat out of the bag, and there was no way to grab it and stuff it back in.

My attempt at living in peace was seen by my mother as a betrayal. She wasted no time in letting me feel her wrath. My life became filled with fear and tension, and I had to walk on eggshells around the rest of my family, the people who should have protected me and cared for me.

It was the beginning of the end of my relationship with my mother and sister.

The Farm

Watching my mother throw me overboard should not have surprised me.

Many people have early childhood memories and can recall the first or second grade, but I can't. I don't remember being hugged or kissed as I made my way out the door to school. It's like I wasn't born until years after that. That can't be the case, so I am stuck with a gap between my birth and the days when my memory comes to life. I've learned that when humans suffer trauma they go into flight or fight mode to seal off the pain. In the process, some painful memories get erased or sealed off to protect us, which probably explains why I don't remember my early years.

The early memories I do recall never involve my mother, father, or sister. Whatever happened in our house the first few years of my life has been wiped away. As I recall my earliest memory, I am wrapped with the enduring love of my grandmother Daisy Viola Wyatt and my grandfather William Forrest Wyatt, my mother's parents. I spent summers and holidays with them on their farm in Lomax, Illinois. Their dairy farm was a safe place for me, a place where I was loved and cared for. Those are the childhood memories that make me warm and happy.

My grandparents had fourteen grandchildren, nine of which were boys, yet I was the only girl who chose to spend her summers on the farm. I feel sorry for my girl cousins because they missed out on the positive, loving moments that helped me grow. Being on the farm allowed me to watch and learn from my grandparents, and they raised me to be authentic, honest, and God-fearing.

The farm was more than just a vacation spot for me. I had lived near my grandparents for most of my early life, and my roots there ran deep. I was born in La Harpe, Illinois on May 29, 1954. My mother, Forrest Darlene Wyatt, spent much of her early life on that land. She was one of five children born to Forrest and Daisy in Lomax, Illinois and was raised on their nearly 300-acre dairy farm with her brothers. It was one of the largest dairy farms in the state, but it seemed cozy and intimate to me.

My father, Billy Merle Harding, was also a farm kid, and that created a bond between him and my mother because they understood how tough farm life could be. They had both strained under the long days and intense labor it took to keep a farm running during sweltering summers and freezing winters. Dad was one of three children born to Tommy and Cora Harding in Blandinsville, Illinois. He was the middle child, born between an older brother and a younger sister. Their parents had a large cattle and hog farm and owned the only gas station in town, a one-pump Shamrock station that sat across the street from their house on the main street. Dad's father ran the gas station, and his mother managed their cattle and hog farm and the business associated with it.

Both of my parents came from wonderful, strong, hard-working American families, forged by the Great Depression and World War

II. Almost no families in that part of the world survived those events unscathed, and mine was no exception. My mother watched three of her brothers being shipped off to fight in World War II. Their youngest brother escaped service only because he died at home from pneumonia at the age of two. Luckily, her other brothers came home from the war and were able to start families and build lives for themselves.

While her siblings were fighting America's enemies, it was up to my mother and her father to run the farm. Farming was the family's way of life, and my mother made sure crops were planted and animals were fed. It was tough work, and she was on the clock from sunup till sundown, 365 days a year. She did the work of three grown men when she could have been going to parties and dancing to the latest songs.

Lomax and Baldwinsville are twenty-two miles apart. That may seem far to city dwellers, but to farm kids in the 1940s and 50s it was all part of the same neighborhood. In those tiny country towns, high school students from all over gathered for proms, dances, graduations, and the like. My parents met at one of those high school dances. They were a beautiful couple, at least on the outside. Dad was handsome, with black curly hair and steel blue eyes. My mother was attractive The final basic human need is the need to procreate as well. She had dark brown curly hair and a wonderful figure for a high school girl, a form sculpted by the hard farm work she did most of her early life.

I never knew how long my mother and father dated. I do know that they were both ready to escape the lives they had been born into. Dad wanted to get out of the house and start his own family, and my mother wanted to flee the grind of working on the farm by becoming a nurse. Sometime after meeting at a dance in the middle of the Illinois countryside, they married and stayed married for twenty-five years.

After they were married, my parents lived close to my mother's parents' farm in Lomax. It seemed my parents would do anything to avoid working on the farm. To support himself and his new wife, my father began driving a milk tanker truck all over the state. I wasn't old enough to understand why he was gone. I only knew that I didn't see Dad much after he started his new job. My mother was a stay-at-home mom to me and my sister until we were old enough to start school, and then she went to work at the Shaeffer pen factory in Fort Madison, Iowa, which was just across the bridge over the Mississippi River.

I would like to say that it was a happy marriage, that my parents' house was full of love, joy, and grace. But if that were the case, this book would never have been written. I have come to learn that most of the years my parents spent together were difficult. As a child, you don't have any context to know if your parents are happy or not or if marriages are supposed to look like the one your parents have. You may not like the way you feel when your parents argue, but you don't know why, and you don't know if similar arguments are happening in the homes of your friends.

It took me decades to understand what was going on between my parents. Whatever love, if that is the right emotion, they felt one night at a high school dance in rural Illinois had long-since vanished. Whatever spark there had been between them had dwindled, and there wasn't enough heat left between them to make a marriage work. The attraction between them must have vanished as quickly as it came. When I was in my forties, my father told me that when he walked down the aisle to marry my mother, he knew he was making the biggest mistake of his life. Those were difficult words for me to hear, but that explained the negative energy that enveloped me as I was growing up. I had been raised by two people who didn't care for each other. They didn't nurture themselves or their relationship, and there was no way they could care for the children they brought into the world.

Despite the tension between my parents, I spent a lot of joyous time with Grandpa and Grandma Wyatt on their farm and in their home in town that was fifteen minutes from the farm. I loved every moment I shared with them.

It helped that I was a tomboy. Working on the farm was right up my alley. There is always something that needs to be done on a large farm, and I loved being my grandfather's shadow and helping him get things done, like milking the cows and planting the fields.

I was thrilled to ride the big farm horse, Jim, who was so gentle that he never bucked any one off. Jim carried me around the fields in and near my grandparents' farm for more hours than I could count.

My grandfather kept his prized bull in a pen, and as I sat on the fence with my boy cousins, they dared me to run across the pen and jump on the fence without the bull catching me. I was afraid, but not so scared that I was going to let my cousins win the bet. I took a deep breath, slid off the fence, and ran like crazy. When I reached the other side without being touched by the bull, I jumped on top of the fence, savored my glory, and smiled at my cousins who hadn't been brave enough to test fate like I had been.

Every summer we had to harvest silage, a green grass that was cut up and stored on the farm. Someone drove a truck behind a tractor as the tractor cut the silage and dumped it into the back of the truck. When the truck bed was full, we drove it behind the barn and dumped the silage into a huge hole that had been dug there. We didn't stop until that hole was full, and the silage that hadn't stuck to our sweaty, sticky skin was fed to cows throughout the year.

My sister never liked the farm as much as I did, and it seemed that she was never there. I do not know why I spent summers with my grandparents and my sister did not, but I do know she never liked the dirt. Even during the few times she was there, she never did the same things I did. While I was busy with farm chores, she preferred being inside and putting her hair in braids or playing with makeup. We were as different as night and day.

Being a tomboy didn't stop me from learning how to do things most girls were expected to. I spent many happy hours in the kitchen learning to cook and bake with Grandma. She made the best cinnamon rolls I have ever eaten, and her loving hands taught me how to knead the dough back and forth until it was ready to be covered with cinnamon and sugar and placed in the oven. When the rolls were done, they were sweet and sticky and baked with all the love Grandma gave me.

All the food we ate was grown on the farm and was fresh and natural. I harvested some of it myself, including picking strawberries with my grandmother, berries that were plump and sweetened by a summer of Illinois sun. She taught me how to make strawberry preserves, and I have never bought anything in a store that tasted as sweet and ripe as the ones we canned ourselves. It is the kind of freshness that cannot be described, only experienced.

We made bread from scratch, kneading each loaf with all the love and skill Grandmother had learned from her mother. I stood next to her, watching, listening, and learning. We made biscuits for breakfast, and when blueberries were in season, we put them in handmade pie crusts and baked them. We always had fresh eggs and milk, another benefit of raising animals on land you owned.

Grandma wasn't just feeding her family. Every week, she fed the people who worked on the farm, including the threshers who helped harvest crops during the summer.

When we were in the mood, my cousins and I jumped into a canoe and went frog gigging on Honey Creek, which cut across the farm. Because I was the only girl, my job was to hold the gunny sack and watch the light brown burlap turn dark as the boys put wet frog after wet frog in it. We carried that damp sack back to the house, where our aunt cut up the frogs and fried them. I never acquired a taste for frog legs, but I will never forget those lazy summer days in Illinois with my cousins.

My grandfather raised beef cattle, and in the nearby town of Stronghurst there was a butcher who cut the meat just the way Grandpa wanted it. After it was packaged, he stored the meat in lockers at the shop. Each one of Grandpa's kids was given their own locker, and they could open it and feed their family any time they wanted to. My grandparents did the same with the pigs they raised, and no one in the family was ever without meat, fresh and free of the hormones that are used in meat raised in modern commercial farms.

It seemed like Grandpa could fix anything with the tools he kept in his wood and metal garage. On the rare occasions where he couldn't repair something with his own hands, he called on his neighbors who came over, and between them they were able to come up with a solution.

When we needed a change of scenery or had to buy one of the few things that my grandparents couldn't grow, we made our way to Ruth's grocery store or Strickland's store for clothes. There was even a movie theatre across the railroad tracks. We could even go to the laundromat and grocery store operated by my Uncle Raleigh and Aunt Effie. They were never able to have children, and they treated us like their own.

After the sun set on the hot, humid Illinois summer nights, the teenagers met under the glow of the town's single streetlight. During one of the few summers that my sister spent on the farm, she wanted to join them. "You can go," my grandfather told her. "But you have to be home when the streetlight turns off at ten." My sister didn't take that warning seriously, and after three or four nights of waiting for her to return, my grandparents had enough. They picked up the only phone in the house, a partly line in the living room, and called my mother. My sister was sent home and never returned to the farm. I couldn't imagine a more severe punishment. I did what I was told because I loved being there and wanted to do the right thing. If I had been told I could never visit my grandparents' farm on the banks of the Mississippi, it would have broken me. It is unlikely I would have recovered.

I wasn't the only one who was showered with love the moment they set foot on the farm. My grandmother made every one of her grandkids feel like they were her favorite. At Christmas, she gave each one of us a hand embroidered gift, and on our birthday, we got a gift with our name sewn on it. Grandma also made lace and quilts by hand, as well as clothes for my Barbie doll. It seemed as if she could make anything with a ball of yarn or a spool of thread, another skill that had been handed down from generations of women who had come before her.

During Christmas, we cut down a tree and decorated it. Every year we had turkey, full of Grandma's homemade stuffing.

When we got sick, Grandma rubbed Vicks VapoRub on our stomachs and gave us something to drink. "Sweat it out," she said.

When winter set in, Grandpa put chains on the tractor, hooked them to a hood from an old pickup truck, and dragged the kids around the fields that had been were mowed flat after the harvest. It may not have been a horse drawn carriage, but it was our version of a winter wonderland.

After my mother's older brother Chet was married, he quickly created a family of six, five boys and a girl. My grandparents decided they should move into town and let Chet and his family stay in their large two-story house on the farm. My grandparents rented a lovely two-story house with a big front porch in Dallas City, Illinois about thirty minutes from the farm. It was across the street from the school that my cousins attended.

Grandma wasn't going to change how she expressed her love just because she moved into town. She said that her grandchildren needed to have a delicious, healthy meal for lunch, and she was going to cook it. Every day for lunch the grandkids walked across the street to eat at her home. It may not have been easy for her, but Grandma enjoyed every second she spent cooking for her family.

Even when Grandma lived in town, she cooked fresh meats, vegetables, and fruit from the farm. She had aluminum plates similar to those that TV dinners came in, and she prepared meals and froze them in a big freezer in their dining room not far from their cuckoo clock. When it was time for lunch, she heated those meals and served them to the people she loved. She also canned meats and vegetables and made homemade preserves, pickles, and salsa, anything you can imagine. There was nothing she could not cook using fresh ingredients they had grown on the farm.

Not much time passed between my grandfather's big laughs. One his quirks was that he liked eating breakfast for dinner. Grandma would have cooked him whatever he wanted, but nothing tasted better to Grandpa after a long day of laboring under the sun than eggs with bacon or sausage. Their dinner table had four chairs and sat by a small stove and high cabinets. A small lazy Susan rested on the table, and the salt, pepper, and jelly that sat on it slowly passed by when Grandpa reached for whatever he needed.

My grandparents were a wonderful, kind, and loving couple. They showed their love for each other every day. Grandpa kissed Grandma on her neck or patted her butt as he walked by. "He thinks he can still do something," she would say. I never heard them fight or argue.

Grandma and Grandpa had a strong faith in God and taught all their grandchildren about His love for us. They may not have gone to seminary, but they understood God's salvation and His plan for us. Every moment of their lives was a devotional on how to live according to God's word. In the summer, when I stayed with them for three months, I sat at Grandma's feet, and she read the Bible to me, cover to cover, a few pages each day. When I heard the last word of Revelations, she flipped back to Genesis and started over from the beginning. In the summer, she walked me across the street to the little white frame Christian Church in town for vacation bible school. I was drawn to God even at such a young age. I could feel something pulling me in and warming my soul. There was no better way to grow up.

Life wasn't perfect for my grandparents, and they faced more than their share of challenges throughout the years. They lost a two-year-old child to pneumonia, but they never forgot about him and celebrated the short time they had with him. Grandma often went to the family plot in Crane Cemetery, which overlooked the farm, and put flowers on his grave. They lost another grandchild to drowning and yet another in a car accident, and those boys are also buried in the family plot. Family was a priority, even when relatives were no longer in their temporal bodies.

My grandmother could do many things, but she never learned to drive, and by the time I was sixteen and had my license, my sister was not coming to the farm anymore. By then, my sister had left home, only to find herself in a marriage with a man who beat her. To help her, my grandparents bought her a baby blue Ford Mustang with a white interior. My stepdad loaded the car onto a truck and delivered it to my sister in El Paso, Texas. When he was unloading the car, he let my sister know how attractive she was. My sister saw what was happening and shut him down quickly.

Sometime later, my sister no longer needed that car, so my grandparents said I could have it, and I used it to drive Grandma around when I was at the farm.

I made friends during the time I spent on the farm. My best friend, Carla, lived in a house with a big game room in the basement. Carla had learned to drive in her parents' tomato fields, and I wonder how many of those plants were sacrificed for her to get her license.

There were many family get-togethers on the farm with my mother's brothers, their wives, and their children. These included my grandmother's famous catfish fries, where we cooked fresh fish the boys caught from the Mississippi River. We fried that bounty in my grandparents' front yard and ate it with fresh corn on the cob, boiled and sweet.

Cooking for our extended family was not an easy task as there were nearly forty of us to feed when we got together. Our family came to the farm for Easter, Thanksgiving, Christmas, and multiple times throughout the year. We were close, and those were wonderful times.

The seeds Grandpa and Grandma Wyatt planted on that farm helped me to be the woman I am today. I could feel how much they loved me, and they were always there for me. The time I spent on the farm gave me the love and support I never felt between the walls of my parents' home. When I had to leave the farm at the end of summer, I counted down the days until I would return. If I had been given the choice to live on the farm fulltime, I would have jumped at the chance.

I do not know why, but we did not see my father's parents often. They weren't out of the picture, but we only visited them two or three times a year. Their home was not warm or welcoming, and it wasn't the kind of place where I created memories like I did at my mother's parents' farm.

That didn't mean I didn't have fun while I was there. Grandpa Tommy Harding was wonderful. Everyone in town liked him. Whenever my mother, my sister, Dad, and I visited, I walked across the street to be with Grandpa Harding at his gas station. He pumped his customers' gas, washed their windshields, and visited with them. He had an icehouse loaded with all kinds of pop and candy, including two of my favorite two things: Orange Crush pop and cold Snickers bars. I sat in the station with him while he played country music on his radio and we sang along. His favorite song was "Hello Walls" by Faron Young, and we crooned it together so many times I knew every note by heart.

Grandmother Harding was cold and standoffish, and she made a lot of rules for the house. My sister and I were not allowed to sit on the "good couch." Some chairs had plastic on them, and I never understood why. Aren't chairs meant to be used? The contrast between my grandparents could not have been more striking.

Life seemed simple in those days, but things began to change. I am not sure why, but we moved to Galesburg, Illinois, which was fifty-seven miles from the farm. It took us an hour to get there by car.

I wonder if my mother was tired of Dad being in the truck all the time. While he was on the road, she had to raise two girls by herself, and that couldn't have been easy. My mother eventually told Dad to get off the road and get a job in town. He obliged and got a job at a department store in Galesburg as a TV repair man. My mother finally became a nurse, and she started working at Cottage Hospital in Galesburg when I was six years old and ready for the first grade. My sister was in the third grade by then, and we walked to school and back home together every day. My mother worked the seven to three shift, and there were times when we got home before she did.

I would have preferred to live next door to Grandpa and Grandma Wyatt, but I was grateful our new house was only an hour's drive from my them. My grandparents drove to see us at least two times a month, if not more. I was thrilled when they arrived. We cooked on the grill and made homemade vanilla ice cream in a hand-cranked machine. The food was delicious, and the company was better.

But seeing my grandparents twice a month could not mend the problems in our home. I could sense things were not great between my parents, even as young as I was at the time. The tension and negative energy in the house became impossible to ignore, and I often heard my parents arguing after I went to bed. Dad hated being a TV repairman and wanted to go back on the road, a fact that did not please my mother.

Dad eventually got his way. He and a friend got a job with a large company hauling freight across the U.S., H.J. Jeffries, which was headquartered in Oklahoma City, Oklahoma. Dad hit the road and left my mother, my sister, and me by ourselves. Dad was gone a lot, sometimes two or three months at a time. On the few occasions he made it home, he did not stay long, usually four or five days. But just because he was home, it didn't mean we got to spend time with him. He spent much of his time in Galesburg at the terminal working on his truck before he left again. He was home during the holidays, but it was more of the same. The visits were short, and he didn't have any time to spend with his family.

After my grandparents passed away years later, it was clear that they had been the glue that held our family together. Not long after they were gone, their kids began fighting, something that never would have happened when Grandma and Grandpa were alive. Their deaths also meant the end to my visits to the farm. If they were not there, what was the point of going? The house wouldn't smell like homemade bread, and there would be no one to pick strawberries with.

My mother didn't give me much, but I will be eternally grateful for the time I had with her parents. They molded me and shaped me in a way she never could.

My grandparents' influence didn't stop when they were gone. Even after he passed, Grandpa found a way to teach a lesson. Grandpa always wanted to be fair, a trait that was especially important because he had so many children and grandchildren. Somewhere along the way, he had loaned my father money to buy a truck, and the loan had not been repaid before my grandparents passed away. Their land was divided equally after they passed, but one of their sons, Chet, had the right to buy all of it, as he had been the one farming it. Chet bought the farm, and the other kids were to get equal shares of that money. But the will stipulated that the money Grandpa had loaned to my father would be deducted from the amount paid to my mother. It was one last way that Grandpa made sure everyone was treated fairly.

The Big Change

When I was nine and ready for the third grade, my mother had enough. Dad seemed to always be in Oklahoma City at the main terminal rather than in Illinois, so my mother decided that we would move to Oklahoma to be with him.

I was devastated, heartbroken, and afraid. I did not know how far Oklahoma City was from Illinois, but I knew it was far enough that I would not see my grandparents as much as I wanted.

Dad had rented a two-bedroom house near an elementary school. We unloaded, but before we had the chance to unpack, Dad left to take a load of pipe somewhere. My mother, my sister, and I were in a strange town in an unfamiliar house full of moving boxes and did not know where anything was except our school. We only knew how to find that because we could see it at the end of the block.

My mother must have been horrified. She had never been away from her parents and family. She enrolled my sister and me in school, me in the third grade and my sister in the sixth. During the day, my mother got in her car and scouted out the town, trying to figure out where we were. She also started looking for hospitals where she could land a nursing job. On the weekends, she put my sister and me in the car and drove until we were lost. The point was to see if we could find our way home. That is how my mother learned how to get around the city.

It did not take my mother long to understand that our house was in the wrong part of town, the not safe part. She was determined to get us out of there and do it quickly. It took moving to four different rent houses for my mother to get us to the part of the town that was safe for us to live and where there were good schools for my sister and me. It was awful to be the new kid at five different elementary schools all within the third grade. Children were not very welcoming to the "new kids," and they made our lives difficult.

The house was close to the hospital where my mother had been hired as a nurse, Hillcrest Hospital. It was a nice three-bedroom, one-car garage house with a big backyard. Mom talked to the owner of the house, Mr. Og, and asked him to let her buy the house as a lease-purchase. He accepted, and we finally had a forever home. My mother didn't move again and spent the rest of her life between those walls.

My mother had accomplished what she set out to do. She had a job, bought a house in a nice part of town, and enrolled me and my sister in good schools. She did all of this while her husband was on the road. After we were settled, my mother called Dad and gave him our new address, and that must have been a shock to him.

I now realize how strong my mother had become. She had found the strength to make sure her children were safe and in a positive environment, even though she was far from her family and her husband was gone most of the time.

My mother didn't get to see her family as much as she wanted to, but my grandparents did travel on the Santa Fe railroad during the winter, when life on the farm slowed down. I was beyond happy when they came, and I know now that my grandmother was watching out for me. Perhaps they knew that our life wasn't as good as it should have been.

The house had hideous carpet, and upon seeing it, Grandpa knew it had to change. He replaced it almost as soon as he got there, a fact that did not sit well with Grandma. "You never buy *me* new carpet," she said.

Despite her hard work, my mother's plan did not succeed. My dad did not come home anymore that he did when we lived in Illinois. She had moved hundreds of miles to be with a man who was never there. The truth is, we should have stayed in Illinois. At least them my mother would have had her parents to help out.

Things were different financially after we moved to Oklahoma City, and not in a good way. On the rare occasions when my dad came home it seemed he had always experienced some unexpected costs on the road. There was never any extra money to give to my mother to pay the bills or to feed us. But he always seemed to have enough money to come home with new Pendleton western shirts, new leather belts, and multiple pairs of expensive cowboy boots. And there was the expense of having a woman in every city, women that expected to be wined and dined. Bless his heart.

My mother caught on after a while, and she did what she had to do to take care of us. When she was waiting for her paycheck and we needed groceries, she heard about a place in downtown Oklahoma City that bought old clothes. She scoured our closets looking for clothes we did not wear anymore or that did not fit us. My sister refused to go to the store with her. I was scared for my mother to go alone so I rode with her. It looked scary and was downtown by the bus terminal. The store bought the clothes, and my mother had money to buy us food. How she did this I will never know. She must have been at the bottom and had to find a way to make things happen.

Time went by. We had good times, good friends, and great neighbors. I enjoyed the elementary school I went to, and my sister's junior high school was just across the street from that, so that made it easy for us. We rode the bus to and from school, and when we missed the one and only bus it was a short fourteen-block walk to get to where we needed to be.

H.J. Jefferies, the company Dad worked for, landed a large contract to haul pipe to build the Alaskan pipeline. The pipe was so long that the trailers had to be custom made. It was going to take fourteen eighteen-wheelers to do the job, and the trucks would be gone three months at a time. They decided to hire outside truckers to complete the project and asked people to bid on the job.

My dad decided he was going to get that contract, and he put in a bid and won. He said it would be a way to make more money and get the family financially sound. He bought fourteen eighteen-wheel semi-trucks and hired thirteen drivers. He drove the remaining one.

Things went from bad to worse. Because Dad owned the trucks, when one broke down the repair costs came out of the money each truck was making and his profits dwindled.

We saw him even less than we did before. When he did come home, he and my mother were distant and arguing. We tried to make the best of it, but that only went so far.

Before it was all over, my parents married and divorced twice. When I was twelve years old and in the seventh grade and my sister in the ninth, our dad announced that he was in love with a woman in Chicago, Joan. She was a waitress who worked in a diner next to the cattle yard there, a place Dad visited every week for a fried ham sandwich. Dad had a thing for redheads, and Joan's flaming auburn hair was right up his alley. He had met her when my mother was pregnant with me. By the time he told us about her, their relationship had been going on for twelve years, and he said he was going to marry her.

I remember watching him walk out of our home with his suitcase. He left without telling me goodbye. After the divorce was final and he was remarried, my sister went to visit him and Joan, but I did not want to go. I was only twelve years old and could not tell what I was feeling, but I knew I was afraid to leave my mother's house to go to my dad's house and spend time with a woman I did not know.

My sister and our mother were locking horns a lot, as most kids do with their parents when they turn fifteen, and my sister needed time away and began spending more time at Dad's house. When my sister visited him on the weekends, she came back and talked about how nice Joan was, what a great cook she was, and how happy our dad was. Joan was genuinely nice to my sister, and they were becoming good friends.

Dad wasn't the only one to jump into a new relationship. Before my mother and Dad divorced, when Dad came home, my mother, my sister, and I would pick him up at the main terminal. In time, all the drivers who worked for my father got to know the three of us. Within thirty days of my dad leaving, one of his drivers called my mother and asked her for a date. He had been watching her when we picked up my dad at the terminal.

My mother agreed to go out with him. When he picked her up for the first time, I had a bad feeling about the man. I could sense he was not the kind of person we needed to be around. Even as a child, I felt his dark energy. At the time I had no idea why I felt things physically and had this strange sixth sense. Today, I know now it is because I am an empath. I pick up energy that other people emit, and I can read people quickly. All people vibrate energy, and that energy can be measured on some machines. Your energy becomes low when you have been traumatized, and when that happens the vibrations you send out attract harmful people and things.

It was the epitome of a whirlwind romance. Within a month, this man asked my mother to marry him. I did not want him to live in our home, and neither did my sister. We told our mother how we felt, but she was determined to do what she felt was best for her. When it became clear my mother was going to have a relationship with the man regardless of how we felt about it, my sister announced that she was moving in with our dad and Joan.

I watched my sister walk out the door with her suitcase in hand to move in with our dad, Joan, and her little girl. That marked the end of what I had known as a family. It may have been tattered, but it was still my family, and I didn't want to see it end. To make it worse, my sister, just like Dad had done, did not say goodbye when she walked away. I felt I should have been able to count on her and had the expectation that she would always be there to help take care of me. I had never known any time away from her since the day we were born. I didn't know how life would continue without us living in the same place.

Maybe I didn't have the right to expect so much from her. She was only a child herself, and she may have had her own issues to deal with. But I needed as many pillars to hold onto as I could find, and her absence devastated me.

When my sister faded into the distance, I was alone with my mother. Maybe we could have built a life together and helped each other grow into better people.

We never got the chance. It wasn't long before my mother brought an enemy into our home. I would soon be on my private island, with no way to escape and no one to rescue me.

Mic Drop Moment

Not long after my sister moved out, my mother had another date with the man who had been a driver with my dad. It was a Friday, and my mother told me the three of us were going to take a short road trip. After they got off work at about 5:00 p.m., I climbed into the back seat of the car, and we headed out.

We drove for what seemed like forever. When it was getting late, we arrived in a town I had never seen before. My mother told me that she and this man I barely knew were going into the big building we were parked in front of. She told me to lock the doors and wait.

As time passed, I got sleepy and fell asleep in the back seat. The next morning, I woke up in our house. I don't remember driving home or going inside. After using the bathroom and brushing my teeth, I walked into our kitchen/dining room. I was not prepared for what I saw.

There he was, sitting at our kitchen table drinking coffee with my mother. He had spent the night at our house, a few feet from my bedroom. My mother told me what happened while I was asleep and why we had taken the car ride. It was illegal in Oklahoma to remarry within six months of getting a divorce. For whatever reason, that man did not want to wait that long to marry my mother, so they agreed to drive to Gainesville, Texas to tie the knot. The fact that my mother had been divorced recently was not an issue there. The big building we had parked in front of was the county courthouse, and they had gone inside and married while I was asleep. That man was now my stepfather.

My mother hadn't said one word to me about marrying him. She never asked my opinion or hinted that she was ready to make such a major life change. I had no idea that when we left on that trip that our family would grow by the time we came home.

I learned many years later that my mother had called my dad and asked him if she should marry the man. That call seemed like the right thing to do. After all, Dad was the father of her children and probably knew the man better than she did. The problem was that my mother didn't listen to what my dad said. He told her absolutely do not marry this man. He said the man was mean, violent, and a horrible alcoholic. He had been to prison for theft and would bring no good to my mother, my sister, or me. My mother heard those words, ignored them, and married the man anyway.

It wasn't long before my stepdad's true colors started showing. He began by finding fault in everything about me. He told my mother that it was too expensive to feed me and pay for my visits to the dentist. He said that I needed to work. He was driving a semitruck at night delivering flowers to florist shops throughout Oklahoma and said he would pay for my care if I went with him on the flower runs and wrote down how many cases were delivered to each florist.

Being alone with him was the last thing I wanted to do, but I wasn't given a choice. My mother told me what I was supposed to do, and that meant helping her new husband. I told her I was scared and did not want to be alone with him. Her response was, "Melanie, you are trying to

make trouble between us. If he says, 'Be a chair,' you need to be a chair."
She dismissed my feelings as if she didn't like a shirt I wanted to buy.

I loved my mother and did not want her to be mad at me. Plus, I was only twelve and didn't know I had the ability and the right to stand up for myself. I thought it was my duty to do what my mother told me to do. The next night I was a good daughter and followed my mother's instructions. I came home from school, did my homework, ate dinner, and at 8:00 p.m., I got in the semitruck with her new husband while he drove across Oklahoma delivering flowers.

At each stop I got out of the truck with the paperwork and marked off the boxes that were delivered. This went on for hours, and I started getting sleepy. I knew by the time we were finished it would be 4:00 or 5:00 a.m., and I would have to get showered, dressed, and go to school. I told my mother's husband I was getting tired and crawled back in the truck to rest, knowing he would wake me at our next stop.

I had no idea how much time passed, but everything was quiet when he pulled over in a rest stop on the interstate. The next thing I knew he forced me out of my sleep by laying on top of me and grabbing my throat with one of his hands. He was trying to force his other hand down my pants.

I fought him and struggled to breathe. I put my arms down to block him from getting inside my clothes, and then he put his hand underneath my blouse. I kicked and screamed to get away. I gathered all my strength and grabbed one of his hands. I put my teeth between his thumb and forefinger and bit down hard, ripping a chunk of flesh away.

I jumped out of the sleeper compartment and sat in the passenger's seat. He slinked into the driver's seat. "If you don't start this truck and take me home right now, I am going to tell my mother what you did," I screamed.

He started the truck and headed to our house. As soon as we arrived, I went to my bedroom. My mother asked him why his hand was bleeding. "I cut it changing a tire on the truck," he said, an explanation that seem to satisfy her. I got dressed and went to school, wondering what I had done to be put into such a miserable situation.

I knew I was at a crossroad but didn't know what I could say to my mother. "Don't you see what he is doing?" I thought. "Why won't you help me or rescue me? You are my mother, and you should put me in a safe place. God, please save me from this pain, this madness."

I told my sister what happened, and we agreed to tell our mother what her new husband had done. We thought our mother would have to listen. We thought she would feel the need to protect us, her flesh and blood, from the man she had brought into our lives.

We were wrong. When were told our mother what our stepfather had done, she chose to protect her relationship with him instead of caring for us.

My stepfather made things worse after I spoke up. From that moment, he began stalking me. I lived in fear every single day. He stared at me during dinner, walked through my bedroom on his way to breakfast, and stood near me as I got ready for school, trying to look down my blouse.

My mother was not willing to protect me and would not believe me, so I did what I could on my own. I moved my bed to the back of my bedroom so I could lean up against the wall and stay awake. That allowed me to watch both of my bedroom doors in case my mother's husband tried to come in while my mother was sleeping.

As you can imagine, because I was staying up all night, my grades began to plummet, but there was no one I could reach out to. Who could I tell, who would believe me if my own mother would not? I was in territory that was becoming all too familiar: alone on an island with sharks circling me.

It couldn't have been difficult for my mother to see the kind of man she had married. He hid bottles of vodka all over the house. They were in the kitchen cabinets, under the kitchen sink, in the garage, and underneath the seat in his truck.

My mother didn't like him being out on the road, so he took a semitruck mechanic job at Hodges Trucking Company in Oklahoma City, and he was home every night.

His new job made my home life even more miserable. When he was on the road, I didn't have to worry about him. I could drop my guard a little. When he pulled in the driveway after a long trip, my mother said, "Melanie, keep your mouth shut. Don't say anything to make trouble." I was a good girl and did what I was told.

By the time I was sixteen years old and driving, my grandmother bought me a 1961 Chevrolet Biscayne from the Shamrock Gas Station by our house for $500. It was one speck of freedom in my otherwise controlled and miserable life. It meant I could escape for a little while as long as I had gas money.

One night, I was helping my mother cook dinner, standing next to her in front of the stove, watching one pan while she was watching another. My stepfather walked into the kitchen and called my mother a "stupid bitch."

Then it happened.

He raised his arm and prepared to slap my mother when my instincts took over. No one was going to hit my mother. I reacted within a millisecond, grabbing a butcher's knife from the wooden knife block on the stove. I stood between my mother and her husband and held the knife to his neck. "Please move one inch so I can slit your throat," I said.

He backed up and the game was on. Neither of them could disregard or deny what had happened. I told my stepfather, "My father may have loved another woman, but he never raised his hand against my mother, and neither will you." By speaking that truth and defending myself, I had unwittingly broken the most important rule in our home: no one was supposed to tell our secrets, either in the home or outside of it.

But sometimes, to protect yourself and to become the person you were meant to be, you have to fight. Sometimes, we have to face the dragons in our lives. Sometimes we have to stand up and fight like we have never fought before. This is what each of us are called to do. To stand up for what is right and good in this world. God is watching us, and He is depending on each one of us to stand up for Him, to be His hands and feet until He comes back.

The Needs

"God dwells within me, as me."
Elizabeth Gilbert, *Eat Pray Love*

When I held a knife against my stepfather's throat, I had no idea I had such strength. I didn't know I had the power to stand up to an aggressor and that I possessed the power to protect myself. The truth is that we all have that power.

In the years that followed, I spent a lot of time and energy understanding why I made certain choices and how I could make better ones. I now understand that many of my choices were the result of the environment I was forced into as a child but that other choices were a matter of biology. I was able to stand up for myself when I had to because I was hardwired to do so, just like you are.

Holding a knife against the man who was trying to take my freedom and made me feel unsafe wasn't as much a decision as it was a reaction that was triggered by one of the most basic needs we all have.

There are three basic human needs, and it's important to remember that if they are not met, or if there are no limits set, humans will act out in unhealthy ways.

The first basic need is the need for **nourishment**. Humans need to eat and drink. Without food and water, we will die within days or weeks. But if the need for nourishment is unchecked, it leads to gluttony. Gluttony can be just as unhealthy as a lack of food and can result in obesity, diabetes, and a host of other problems.

The second basic need is the need for **protection**. We all need to feel safe and secure, that we will be able to survive the moment and make it home safely. When we don't feel protected, it can lead to aggression. This is what I felt when I saw my stepfather about to strike my mother. My sense of security was threatened, and I lashed out to save my mother and myself.

The final basic human need is the need to **procreate**. The survival of our species depends on our ability to bring forth another generation. But when left unchecked, our need to procreate can lead to lust, and this can be expressed in unhealthy activities such as addiction to pornography or sex.

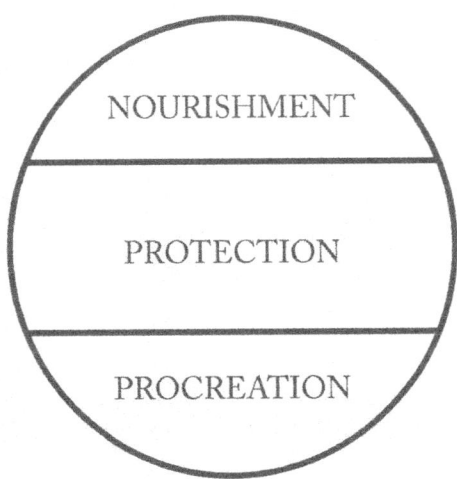

Holding a knife against my stepfather's neck wasn't the only time I acted out of a need for self-preservation. There are four times in my life when I acted so aggressively that after the moment was over, I thought, "Who was that person?" I felt shame and embarrassment because I did not know that inside of me there was such a strong need to protect myself.

Each time I related aggressively to a dangerous situation, I was alone or felt isolated. I was fighting to stay physically safe because no parent/husband/significant other was protecting me. I was driven by my basic desire to survive when I felt I was in physical danger from another human being. Now that I understand that, I no longer feel shame or embarrassment about my actions. Those moments of intense aggression make sense. My behavior was valid and called for because people were trying to physically harm or kill me.

Not everyone handles threats to their physical safety the same way. Perhaps my mother was protecting herself by not rocking the boat when my sister and I told her what her new husband had done. I later learned that my stepfather had threatened to kill her if she ever left him. There were other issues as well. "I have sexual problems due to your father, and your stepfather has to put up with them," she told me. Maybe my mother was still a frightened little girl doing her best to stay safe. Maybe she wasn't healthy enough to care for children. Plus, she didn't grow up in a time when people talked about depression, and there were no support groups for people with mental health issues. She might have done the best she could with the cards she had been dealt.

When my sister felt threatened, instead of acting aggressively toward her attacker, she protected herself by removing herself from the danger. At sixteen years old, she married the neighbor boy who was three years older than she was. He was drafted into the Army and was stationed in Wildflecken, Germany. They had been dating, and when he came home on leave, he asked her to marry him and go back to Germany with him. She agreed, and that union allowed her to put as much distance between herself and our family as she could.

That was her way of escaping the dysfunction in our family. From that moment until the writing of this book, sixty-seven years later, my sister never moved back to Oklahoma and calls ten rolling acres in California her home. I now understand why she made that choice. When you leave a place where all you know is the trauma and dysfunction, you do not have to face that pain again. Leaving makes your life is much easier. You escape it all. You put your trauma in a box, shut the lid, and never have to face it again. My sister did visit Oklahoma a few times over the years, but she left almost as soon as she came. Perhaps the pain is still too strong for her to endure.

There might be another dynamic that made it difficult for my sister to face the fact that our mother had chosen her marriage over her daughters. My sister and my mother were very close and had a special connection, but I never knew why. One reason might be that while I was spending summers on my grandparents' farm, the two of them were alone. Maybe that time together helped them forge something I would never be a part of. Whatever the reason, they shared a bond I never had with either of them.

Because of that connection, I thought my sister would want our mother to know the truth. I expected my sister would go with me and tell my mother about what a horrible person my stepfather was. If we told our mother what her husband had done, she would believe my sister at least, and our mother would get rid of him.

When that didn't happen, I spent years in therapy and working on myself peeling back layers to arrive at the core of who I am. I wanted to find out what happened to me in my childhood. I struggled with what my mother had done and why she valued a new husband more than her children. My amazing therapist, Dr. Gary Cone, shared with me that my mother probably didn't know what she was doing. He said sometimes a mother offers up her daughter sexually to a husband when she has sexual problems of her own. It is not something the mother does consciously or intentionally. My mother might have been mentally ill and ignoring the abuse that was right in front of her may have been her way of protecting herself. Looking at things from that perspective helped me to understand that my mother's actions may not have been conscious choices. Maybe she was suffering from problems that she was not sharing with me or anyone else.

When I was in my thirties, an amazing therapist came into my life, Dr. Pamela Walker. I was having nightmares about being held by the throat by a man who was standing over me. The memories of my stepfather had come back. Dr. Walker began to work with me on healing.

She taught me that how we protect ourselves can sometimes be harmful. She talked to me about forgiveness and how it releases you. For several weeks, she brought up the idea of forgiving my stepfather, and I objected strongly. "I cannot forgive my stepfather," I said more than once. During one session she stopped me and asked, "Melanie, do you know what forgiveness means?"

"Yes. It means you have to act as if it never happened, and I cannot do that."

"No. That is not what forgive means. It means you forgive the person so you are released from the anger and resentment. You are not tied to it anymore, but *you never forget.*"

A wave of freedom came over me. I got it. At that moment, I understood I could make a choice. Now that I knew the danger and dysfunction certain people create, I could choose not to be around them anymore. My mind had been trying to protect me by holding on to anger towards people who had harmed me so that I would avoid them, like a child who fears a stove after being burned by it. That protection came at a cost. It sapped my energy and my joy and put me in a prison. Letting go of the harm that people had caused me, but not forgetting what they had done, freed me to live a fuller life.

My Other Family

I may not have felt a connection with my mother or sister, and my stepfather may have been a predator, but I wasn't without love. I sought out people who shared my values and bonded with people who loved and cared for me.

I still have the red Bible that Reverend Hamm of Hillcrest Christian Church gave me on the day he baptized me, April 27th, 1964. I was ten years old and had joined Pastor's Class, a yearlong study about what God's word says about baptism. I ended the year by being baptized on Easter Sunday.

Even at such a young age, I felt a strong calling from God. I knew it was my duty to be washed and become a member of God's church. Reverend Hamm immersed me in the water in a glass baptismal that was high enough above the pulpit in the middle of the church so that the whole congregation could witness my transformation. I was so short that he had to put a box for me to stand on the bottom of the baptismal.

Reverend Hamm asked me the questions every soul has to answer before they are baptized: Do I believe in the Father, the Son and the Holy Spirit? Was I willing to confess my sins? I said yes, and with his hand on my tiny back he submerged me.

I will never forget his words when I came out of out of the water. He said, "Go and walk in the newness of life." I was infused with something I had never felt before, something magical and wonderful. I had knocked at the door, and God opened it and welcomed me with unconditional love and acceptance.

I was led to that church almost as soon as we moved to Oklahoma City. I hated living there. I missed my grandparents and their farm. As far as I was concerned, their farm was Heaven on Earth, and nothing in our new home could compare to that.

Because of the love and support I felt in the church my grandmother had taken me to during the summers I spent on the farm, when I arrived in Oklahoma City and was unhappy and afraid, I knew if I went to church, I would be comforted. I also knew that if I went to church, I would be going alone. My father was on the road in his truck three to four months at a time. My mother worked every other Sunday. My older sister had no interest in God or anything spiritual. To this day she is proud to tell you she is a confirmed atheist and prouder that she married a man who shares that belief.

After we moved into our house, my sister and I were in the back seat of the car as our mother was driving to a nearby grocery store on a Saturday. We passed a building with a sign out front that read, "Hillcrest Christian Church."

That sign gave me hope, and I knew that's where I would be going. That Sunday my mother was working, but I got up and walked the four blocks to the church by myself. I entered through the back door, and a woman welcomed me. She asked me how old I was so she could take me to the right Sunday school class. I felt so welcome that I stayed for church and sat on the second row on the righthand side in front of the pulpit. It was so peaceful that I walked to that church every Sunday.

Reverend Hamm and his wife noticed that I was there every week. They also noticed I came alone and walked out the back door of the church as soon as service was over.

They took me under their wings and never asked me questions about my family or why I always came by myself. I suppose they knew something had to be going on at home if a young child was attending church by herself.

I didn't know it at the time, but I have come to know that in God's perfect timing, He will reveal to you the answer to every question, concern, or heartache you experience. The amazing thing you realize is that all the painful things you suffered were part of God's plan. It takes time and a deep relationship with God, but when we grow spiritually, we get an awareness, a wide-angle lens view of our life and begin to see how everything, the good and the bad, fit together as it was supposed to according to God's divine wisdom. I experienced excruciating pain at the time, but I was also seeing examples of unconditional love in the way Reverend Hamm and the members of his flock treated me.

It also took me years to understand why my family didn't accept my decision to attend church and why they never offered me any support. In 2020, my pastor began teaching a Bible study called Loaves & Fishes. He told us the lesson for the year was called, "The Work of the Holy Spirit Today." A small, still voice inside me said, "Go."

I have learned to listen to that voice, and I went to the next meeting of Loaves & Fishes. The pastor shared about how he felt when he got saved, when he reached out and grabbed God's hand and said "Yes." He said that he went to the work the next morning, his secretary saw him and said, "You look different. What has happened?"

The Holy Spirit spoke to me at that instant. He said, "That's the reason your birth family did not accept you. After you were baptized, they recognized that you looked different. They sensed the energy of the Holy Spirit living inside you."

God also told me, "I will give you the family I have chosen for you and bring them into your life."

My pastor's willingness to share truths about his life and experiences awakened and healed me. My family's choices made sense to me after he spoke. His words answered the "why" question I had been asking for so long.

The only time my mother, father, and sister came to a service at Hillcrest Christian Church was when I told them I wanted to be baptized. They came that Sunday, which was Easter Sunday, but never again. After that, each of them in their own way and on their own timing said to me, "You think you are better than us."

My sister tried to make me feel small for having faith. She told me, "I do not believe in God. He is not real." During my senior year of high school, after I expressed my strong desire to get a college degree, my father said, "You don't need a college education. You just need to marry a man, and he will take care of you." My parents repeatedly told me they were not going to help me once I was out of school. "You are on your own. You just need to get married. You don't need to go to college," were the phrases my parents told me as often as they could.

Fortunately, even though my biological family didn't believe in me, other people around me were supportive and loving. They encouraged me to go in the direction of my dreams. God's miracles came through the hands of His people and institutions, despite the unwillingness of my family.

I learned that God is good all the time, every time, forever and always. Keep your faith strong and engaged and forever connected to your source energy, God.

Layers

"Kindness when freely given is unconditional love."

Saying a few words about my healing fails to describe the hard work that I put into growing as a human. It took me twenty-five-plus years to get to the core of who I am and to appreciate that I am more than a physical body. It took me a long time to understand I have a soul and spirit. I cannot say it has been easy, but I can say it has been rewarding to live a happy and peaceful life. I am grateful for my growth and for my freedom, a feeling that has taken me most of my life to find.

I didn't walk this path alone. Many amazing people joined me on this journey and guided me to where I needed to be. Some of them were only in my life for a short time, while others worked with me for years.

Regardless of how many people are in your life, *you* have to do the hard work to heal. Many people aren't willing to do that, and that is why they don't grow. A wonderful therapist I went to for five years told me that during his thirty-plus year of practice few patients stayed as long as I did. Many people ran away from the issues they needed to confront instead of working on themselves.

I asked him why so many people did not stay, why they left before their work was done. "Because it's too hard," he said.

My response was, "How could they not stay?" When I started therapy, I couldn't breathe anymore. The pain of my life was killing me. I couldn't imagine that anyone would choose to stay in a painful, soul-crushing place when people were willing to give them roadmaps to peace and serenity.

I didn't care what the cost was. I was determined to build a better life for myself. I felt better after each week, each month, and each year as I started my path to healing and recovery. The fog was lifting. Inner understanding was coming.

I learned a lot about my past and the choices I had made. What some people would judge as my "mistakes" were really my teachers. I could feel inner healing taking place. I was changing and I knew it.

As the years went by, I grew as far as I could with one therapist and was ready to go the next level. When change was needed, God put the next healer on my path. They showed up out of nowhere to teach and guide me through the next phase of healing, understanding, and growth. I did not ask for these people to come into my life. I did not search a directory, go online, or ask for recommendations. Our paths crossed through the strangest ways. That was how God took care of me when I needed Him to.

Although I had moved further down the road to becoming a healthy human being, I still had a lot of work to do. I was in a lot of pain, and that pain drove me to make poor decisions and life choices. Somehow, my broken spirit thought that these choices would alleviate my pain and fix everything.

They did not. In fact, my choices drove me deeper into my pit of pain and personal hell. They often put me in incredibly dangerous situations. When I faced another horrible decision, I would think, "Okay, this one will surely work. This time my choice will be a good one."

I have learned not to be judgmental and hard on myself. I was making decisions out of pain and fear. I was not connecting with my spirit, soul, or God's voice, all of which were inside me. And, perhaps worse of all, I neglected my intuition. When you are quiet enough to hear it, when you sit in silence, you will hear your intuition. You will feel a knowing and a connection as to what the right decision is.

But to get to that point, you have to have focus, skill, and patience. I did not possess those qualities earlier in my life. When I was younger and could have used some extra time to think about a decision, my thought was, "Wait for anything? Are you kidding me?" I was running around each day at Mach 10 with my hair on fire. Just to be clear, that nervous energy was not from drugs, alcohol, or any other substance. It was from the turmoil that had been forced on me during my childhood.

Pain, trauma, and fear affect not only your emotional state, but also your body, and if you live with untreated trauma long enough your health will suffer. This was compounded by how I handle conflict and stress. When emotional pain happens to me, I take it in internally, into my body. I get physically ill.

Other people react differently when they suffer verbal, emotional, or physical abuse. Some start shopping excessively. I never knew that was a way people responded to pain until a dear friend of mine showed me her bedroom closet. It was full of beautiful designer clothes covered in plastic, all of them with the tags still on them. There were boxes and boxes of unworn designer shoes and more handbags that most women will own in a lifetime. I stared at all the beautiful and expensive things stuffed in that closet.

She looked at me and said, "I've never worn any of these. I bought them to get a release."

Buying expensive clothes didn't appeal to me. I swung another way. I expressed my pain in ways that impacted my physical body. I took control of my food intake and weight. Instead of excessive eating or becoming bulimic, I quit eating and exercised as much as I could. My hunger disappeared and excessive running, running, running ensued. I ran five miles a day, eight on Saturdays. When running six days a week wasn't enough to escape my pain, I added cycling, aerobics, and weight-lifting into the mix. Exercise can be healthy, but I turned it into pain.

When I became emotionally stronger and healthier, I was able to look inside myself and discover what the person inside my physical body was about. I examined the deep pain that was driving all of my choices, choices that were bringing me more pain. It was a vicious cycle that kept me in a pattern of despair and hurt.

My hope is that you can follow me on this journey and that sharing my story may help you on your path. You will fall and stumble, but trust me, you will get back up as I did, even though I did not always get up pretty. But I dusted myself off and learned from those experiences. I moved forward.

Lessons in the Scars

"If I don't have red, I use blue."
Pablo Picasso

God loves each of us and is waiting for us to invite Him into our lives. He wants us to nourish a personal and intimate relationship with Him each and every day.

But that doesn't mean life will always be fair, and there are times you will suffer and things will leave you tattered and bruised. My scars tell a story. They are reminders of times when life tried to break me but *life failed*. My scars guided me to become the woman I am today. Without the debilitating trauma I endured, I would not have been in enough pain to reach out for help or to lean into help when it arrived. Every relationship in my life, including my family, lovers, friends, and co-workers, was part of God's plan for me. Each one of those relationships moved me a little closer to where I needed to go, sometimes an inch, sometimes a mile.

After I made one of many bad decisions about relationships, I spent a night sprawled on my bedroom floor sobbing and cried out to God. "God, please, please help me," I said. "I don't care what it takes. I want to be so close to you that I could lay my head on your lap and rest. I want that as soon as possible."

After I prayed those words, it was clear God heard them, and He answered me. He started placing relationships in my life, one after another. None of them lasted long. They were short and quick, but every one of them was important. I learned the lessons those people were sent to teach me, and I grew in a short period of time.

The other part of these relationships was that each one was more painful than the last. As I was going through this, God watched me and knew exactly how much I could take. He knew when I was getting too close to the edge, and He always sent in an angel when I needed to step back.

When I was fearing for my life in Paris, having followed a man I barely knew there and was uncertain how I would make it home, a woman I had seen on the hotel elevator showed up out of nowhere. After seeing how I was being treated, she knocked on my door and said, "Don't worry. I'll feed you." It was God's voice coming from a woman's mouth.

That is how the God of my understanding takes care of us when we are in danger. He uses other people, His angels, to rescue us. When you need them, angels arrive with food, shelter, a job, or even a car. One of my angels gave me an entire company.

It's easy to find memories that you thought you had forgotten. Get quiet. Sit in your favorite chair or couch. Snuggle up with your comfy pillows or wrap yourself in a soft blanket. Turn off your radio, TV, and cell phone. Get rid of the distractions and be comfortable and quiet in your safe place.

Then scroll back in your mind, going as far back as you can remember. Think of times you were in pain and faced a difficult situation. Remember what happened. Who showed up almost magically and turned your life around? When you needed it the most, who brought you food, shelter, a job, or safety? After it was over, you asked, "How did that happen? I didn't know that person."

Times like that are when God is watching over you while you walk the plan He has for your life. It's His way of putting you on a path to growth, back on your journey, and bringing you home to Him and His love.

Sometimes, angels will speak to you in ways you might never expect. On May 22, 2019, I was watching *The Voice*. I enjoy this TV show because it's a singing competition, and music is a part of who I am. A young woman performed a song she had written herself:

> *Maybe you didn't know*
> *Maybe I was not enough*
> *But, Oh God knew.*
> *Maybe my shine was too bright.*
> *Maybe you were afraid of my light*
> *But, Oh God knew*
> *God knew, the angels knew*
> *Maybe your pain was too deep*
> *Maybe your journey back was too much of a leap*
> *But, Oh God knew*
> *But, Oh God knew*
> *The angels knew*
> *Angels sang for the joy of a child wayward bound,*
> *coming home*
> *God knew.*

The song spoke to me because it touched the truth of my life, which has had so many twists and turns and has been so painful so often. My tendency is to suck it up and not tell anyone, but I learned the hard way that not talking about my pain leads me to dangerous places. Holding in my agony and silencing my story almost destroyed my life.

That approach made me hit bottom and forced me to find help in an inpatient treatment center. From one of my dark places, I learned that telling the truth and getting professional help would set me free. What I didn't know what that freedom was an expensive thing, and it ultimately cost me everything, including my family.

Once I made the commitment to repair the damage that had been done to me and to become healthier, I didn't hold back. I did everything I could to grow. It never occurred to me that people, especially my family, would not want me to be healthy and that they would do what they could to hinder my growth. At times, they tried to sabotage it. Fortunately, other people stepped up and helped me along the way.

10,000 Miracles

I had taken a job as an executive assistant for a corporation in Norman, Oklahoma and worked for the President and CFO but had not been there long. The company was in a two-story building, and the main copy machine was downstairs. One morning I walked down to the copy machine to make copies when a girl from the accounting department walked up and said, "There is something different about you. What are you are doing?"

I was not sure what she meant, but something nudged me to give her an answer. "Every Thursday on my lunch hour I walk a block down to the church where they have a teaching time and lunch," I said. "It's called Loaves & Fishes."

I invited her to come with me. She went, and we became good friends. Those kinds of things have continued to happen throughout my life. People see a light inside me and want to know where it comes from. What surprises me was that I feel it, but I did not know anyone could see it.

The company I worked for was a family-owned corporation, and it was a warm and amazing place to work. The owners made all the employees feel like we were part of their family.

I got the job out of the blue after being interviewed by a head-hunter in town. It wasn't a smooth transition. There was a difficult learning curve. My boss never had an assistant and did not know how to interact with me so that we could work as a team. It took us a while to soften our rough edges and work together. After we learned our roles and how to help each other, we, along with the CEO and his assistant, became a force, a well-oiled machine. The four of us had a rhythm.

We needed to be a great team, because the company was expanding rapidly. When I was hired, the family business had fourteen locations. When I left, they had more than fifty stores across the United States.

We were proud of what we were achieving. We worked hard because we were a part of a strong, successful team, and we didn't want to let each other down.

The company grew so large that management decided it was time to go public. We were overjoyed, and the company gave us the opportunity to buy stock. Being included in opportunities like that was one of the reasons we felt like family.

As the company began to file the papers, documents, and requests to go public, the plan was presented to the Board of Directors when a glitch appeared. All executive management employees, including me, had to have college degrees. That was a problem because some of the employees had not earned degrees. I was one of them.

The company could not fire us, which meant they had to find a solution, and they came up with a great one. They told us the company would pay for each of us to finish our college degrees. They didn't care if we majored in basket weaving. We just had to earn a valid college degree. The details were up to us.

It was welcome news. When I was in my twenties, I took my basic classes at a junior college close to where my then husband and I lived, much to his dislike. But when my funds ran out, I wasn't able to finish my degree.

That always bothered me. I wanted a college diploma hanging on my wall. When I saw a degree in someone's office, I admired and respected them and their ability to complete that goal. I had that desire inside me, but I didn't have a way to make it happen. My spirit was willing, but my bank account was weak.

After the company told us they would pay for our degrees, I jumped at the chance. I enrolled at the University of Oklahoma to take the classes I needed to graduate. I scheduled classes around my work hours, either during my lunch hour or after work. It was working well until it became difficult to find classes that fit my work schedule. After you take your required classes, some of the elective classes you need are only offered once a semester. Many of my required classes were offered only on a Monday, which is often the busiest day of the week at a company, especially a retail business.

I told my boss about the challenge I was having. "Talk to your college counselor and see if there is any other way you can get this finished without taking classes during office hours," he said.

When I talked to my college counselor, she said, "Melanie, the goal of any college is to keep you enrolled so that you pay the most tuition possible. You need to graduate as quickly as possible. I am going to tell you how to get this done. I was a professor at Southern Nazarene University, and they have a program that would be great for you." She gave me the name and phone number of person to call at SNU, which was in a suburb of Oklahoma City, and we scheduled a meeting. When we met, the counselor told me about the school's graduate program, how long it took, and that it was only in the evenings. He also told me the total cost was $10,000.

I was a single mother raising a son barely making ends meet, and that number was way beyond my budget. It looked like I would have to drop out of school and find another job.

The next day, my boss asked me how the meeting went and what I found out. I told him about the meeting and the $10,000 it would cost to complete my degree. I also told him I didn't have the money.

He walked out of his office and went down the hall to the accounting manager's office. Within a few minutes, my boss walked up to my desk and handed me a check made out to SNU for $10,000.

I couldn't believe what had happened. Why were these good things happening to me? Nothing in my life had prepared me for that.

After some reflection and prayer, I believed that God had stepped in and made it happen. I took the check to the university, completed my classes, and graduated with honors. The diploma I had always admired and respected hangs on my wall. I earned it because God sent an angel to take care of me.

Now or Later

There is a saying: "You can either deal with it now or deal with it later because it's not going away." Our hurt, fear, and pain stay inside of us. If we do not deal with these when they come up, they manifest themselves in harmful ways.

Those feelings and emotions can force us to stuff them deep inside of us. People with unresolved pain often start drinking, doing drugs, developing issues with food, shopping excessively, or having anger issues. The list goes on and on as to how trauma distorts our behavior and impacts our life and relationships.

Life doesn't have to be that way. There is hope. God has a wonderful, amazing life waiting for each of us. Some of us never find those lives. Some people stop halfway and say, "This is good enough." But there is so much more, and they would find it if they would keep going, even if it is only an inch at a time.

Does that mean life will be perfect? No. Will difficult things still happen in your life? Yes. But when you know that you have an amazing lifeguard beside you, it changes everything. You view the circumstances of your life differently. You can swim off the island and not worry about tides, currents, or sharks. You don't fear them, you know God is working on them, and you go about your day. I trust God to watch over me, and when He sees Satan trying to take me down, He intervenes.

I pray the following prayer each morning before I leave my house: "I love you, Lord. Surround me with a hedge of protection. Surround me with angels. Keep all evil people, negative people, and mean people away from me. In your divine wisdom for my life, bring me today only what is in my highest and best good. Tell my Holy Spirit what I can do for you today."

That's the life preserver that allows me to swim off my island and into the world where Satan is in control for now. But God is my 800-pound gorilla running interference for me every day. My job is to let Him do it. I suit up, show up, and put one foot in front of the other. It is so freeing, so peaceful, so calming to let go of control. Doing that gives me the freedom to continue growing and learning. Life is no longer the painful daily struggle it used to be.

This has given me a peace that passes all understanding. It took me a long time to understand this because it took me a long time to become teachable. I wasn't able to change until God reached down from heaven and scooped me up.

What has happened in my life since then is unimaginable, unfathomable, and amazing. I now have the vision and wisdom to understand that God was saving me. He had been doing this my entire life, but it took me dying to understand that.

My flesh, my sarx (that word comes from Paul's Epistles in the Bible and means the flesh) was blinding me. It was making my decisions. I was listening to my human shell instead of my inner voice, my intuition, God's voice.

I paid the price for trying to be the leader. That choice caused me a lot of pain and despair. It also taught me a valuable lesson: The minute I try to make something happen, I'm in trouble.

The Reaction

Even though I had a successful job and had earned a college degree, I learned that I may not have had as much freedom as I thought I did. There is a pivotal point when the response system in our brain is triggered. It happens to all of us when the amount of pain and fear is so intense that breathing becomes difficult. At that point, our brain releases a chemical that produces the "fight or flight" response. Some people call it the "knee-jerk" reaction.

At that point, our soul, our will, reason and emotions know we are in trouble and danger. They take over to make sure we are safe.

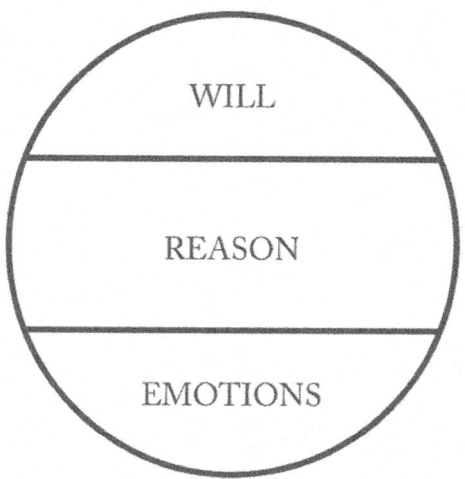

The will is where we receive input from our reason so that we can make decisions. The reason processes this stimuli and judges whether that input needs to be acted upon. The emotions are where bodily stimuli are presented to the mind (the soul).

When someone is not protecting you, your will, reason, and emotions work together to make sure you are safe. The problems come when you are making decisions based on something other than God's will.

When I was having the most problems, I was not waiting for God to bring me my highest and best good in His perfect timing. I made choices from my humanness. I was taking control of making the life I wanted, the one I believed would make me happy, instead of waiting for God's divine wisdom.

I should have read the signs that my choices weren't working. But I was in so much pain that all I could do was to try and make it go away. I thought I could treat the symptoms and that would make me healthy. I thought intense exercise would heal me. Every day I woke up at 5:00 a.m. and ran five miles. I was done before my now ex-husband and our infant son woke up.

When I finished my run, I came home, woke my family, and fixed my husband's lunch. After he was out the door, I fed my son then got ready for work. After a full day of work, I went to the gym and worked out again. I put my headphones on and cranked up the music while I was exercising so I didn't have to listen to my thoughts.

If done in a positive way, exercise can be a healthy thing. But I was working out for the wrong reasons. I was running away from my pain, and my body paid the price. To share with you how excessive and how distraught I was becoming, I am 5'5" and at my lowest I weighed eighty-six pounds and was severely anemic.

Anyone looking at me could see that something was wrong, but I could not see any of this. I was on the inside of me. I had no ability to comprehend how deep my pain and trouble ran.

With some more work, I was able to peel back a few more layers and get closer to my true self. I learned that I am codependent, a disease that creates an internal pain so intense people who suffer from it can barely breathe or think clearly. I may have looked cool and calm on the outside, but on the inside, I felt like a hamster racing on a wheel. To make it worse, I thought if I went a little faster, I could get to the end and make it stop. I didn't understand that the wheel would only stop when I got off of it. There was no way to win the race I had created for myself. There was only more work that led to nowhere.

If you are codependent, you don't dive into a bottle or pills, you jump into an alcoholic or addict. You become a rescuer and are convinced you can help lost people put their boats back on course. The craziest thing is that I had no awareness, zip, nada, that I was doing this, and I had no idea where this came from.

The truth is, my mother had taught me, groomed me, mirrored her behavior to me, and that created this horrific disease. She seared it into my psyche when I was twelve after she married a violent alcoholic and brought him into our home. She gave me a graduate class on how to become codependent. I watched how she crumbled and lost her strength under the verbal abuse and cruelty of that man, and I became an excellent student. I graduated with honors, without even knowing I had enrolled.

I doubt that my mother knew what she was doing. She was probably as blind to her issues as I was to my codependency, and timing may have played an important role in how my mother's behavior impacted me.

One of my therapists told me that if my mother had chosen to marry this man when I was eleven or thirteen it would not have had the same impact that it had when I was twelve. He said at the age of twelve, a child's brain is growing and changing, transitioning from functioning like a child to thinking like a young teenager. There is something crucial about that year, and things that happen when a child is twelve can have a greater influence than those that occur a few months earlier or later.

When I found myself in harmful situations over and over during my difficult years, I had no idea, no thought in my mind, no understanding of what was going on with me. I didn't understand that the cause of my pain was *me*. I was the disease. I was committing the same behaviors that my mother had. Because of what she taught me, I allowed myself to have relationships with men who had the same dysfunctions as my stepfather, and I suffered the same abuse my mother had experienced.

Here's one version of how this played out in my life, over and over. Men would show up in my life and ask me out. All these men had one thing in common: they had at least one disease of their own which they had not treated. It's possible they were unaware that they were sick, although it was probably obvious to most of the people around them (except me, of course).

I have no doubt that my actions and beliefs brought these dysfunctional people into my life. We put an energy or vibration into the world. We attract people that are vibrating at the same energy level as we are.

Once you are healthy, your vibrations change, and so does the quality of people you bring into your life.

Within a month or so, said "man" would ask me to marry him. Escalating a new relationship in such a short period of time *should* have been a red flag to me. But in my mind, if the man said, "I love you," wrote a love song, and sang it to me while playing his guitar, he must really be in love.

While I was listening to these musical masterpieces, I thought, "This could work. We could make a family together. His children, my son, and the two of us could be a family." All of the signs that read "Dead End Ahead" disappeared under a blue cloudless sky.

I was desperately trying to create the family I wanted to have. I kept trying to put the pieces of my broken life back together over and over again, not knowing they would never become the beautiful picture I imagined. Every time a new man showed up in my life, I thought, "This time it will be right. This time it will be true love." It never occurred to me that I had to change how I viewed relationships, including my definition of love.

My sponsor at the time was Paula D. When I left an inpatient treatment center to deal with my codependency, one of the things my facilitator told me was that within thirty days of returning home that I had to attend a CODA meeting, group for people suffering from codependency. I followed that advice and looked for one as soon as I got home.

In my town there were no CODA meetings, so I called my facilitator, and he said I should find an Al-Anon meeting. I found one not far from where I lived and went to a Saturday morning meeting. I was terrified to walk through that door, but I was more scared not to. I was horrified that if I did not do what my facilitator asked me to do, I would fall back into my pain. I walked in, found a chair on the side of the wall, and sat by myself. The meeting started. I listened.

Halfway through the meeting, there was a coffee break. One thing I have learned about alcoholics is they drink gallons and gallons of coffee. I don't like coffee, so I sat in my chair and watched and listened to the people in the room. Two women were sitting together, laughing, smiling, and looking very happy.

"I don't see how any of this is funny or laughable," I thought. But if they thought the meeting was amusing, I was going to find out why. After the meeting I was drawn to one of the women. I introduced myself and learned that she, Paula, had had been in the program for more than twenty years. We talked, and I asked her if she would be willing to be my sponsor. I am thankful she said yes.

My eyes started to open after I met Paula. It was her guidance that nudged me awake and made me realize if I fell for another love song, I would slide down that slippery slope and start all over again. She taught me that recovery isn't going to happen in a flash. That's why people are told to stay in the program. Healing takes more than months. It takes years.

A good sponsor will look at things over the long haul. Many sponsors tell the people they sponsor that they cannot go out a date for one year, or they tell them to buy a house plant. If they keep the plant alive for a year, they can have a date. Many plants have been sacrificed while people are waiting to become healthy enough to go on a date. But having to buy another house plant is much better than having to put your life back together after another messy and needless breakup.

The Girls with the Green Dots

Paula must have had a sixth sense about what I needed to work on. Maybe she had done so much work on herself that she was able to pick up on my energy and read my situation. Paula's ex had been violent, and she had learned to read people to stay safe. She was a double winner: she went to Al-Anon and AA.

When Paula started sponsoring me, she and I went to an Al-Anon meeting near her home. The building was set up like an old shotgun house, and to get from the front entrance to the room where our meeting was being held, we had to walk through a room where an AA meeting was taking place.

I couldn't help but notice a lot of the men in the AA meeting were staring at us. Paula said, "Melanie, these men see the green dot on your forehead. That's why they will come after you."

"What green dot?" I asked.

"They can tell you are new to the program, and they know they have to move quickly and ask you out on a date before you learn too much." It was like I had to learn a new language in order to navigate my way to a healthy life.

She was right. I was fresh meat to men who were struggling with their own diseases and recovery.

I attended meetings on a regular basis and was committed to becoming a healthier person. I learned that all of my failed relationships, short lived as they were, even the marriage that lasted only one day, were part of my recovery. As painful and destructive as those relationships were, once I learned to use them as examples of what not to do, they became powerful teachers. They taught me more and more about who I was and how I could grow, heal, and move to the next level.

My experience with men was not uncommon. Many women in the program had gone through the same thing. It happened so often that women came up with an expression about the men in the program who are trying to catch a woman there. It goes like this: "If you would just lower your expectations, we could be happy."

The sad truth is that I've been there, done that. I'm even sadder to say I've been there more than once.

I am going to cut to the chase. I am about to teel you how ugly my codependency looked, and here is your opportunity to judge me. Use your time wisely. You only get ten minutes. Enjoy it. Relish judging another human who was learning about life. Your time starts now.

Tick. Tick. Tick.

Your time is up. Now move into understanding, compassion, and empathy. Think about times you had difficult learning experiences. What did you do? What did you feel? What did you learn?

If your heart was open, you perceived God's incredible compassion and love for you. Just you. You didn't think of anyone else at that moment. It seemed like the only important things in the universe were you, God, and His incredible love flowing to you.

After having moments where you were bathed in God's grace despite your shortcomings, why would you judge me? Why would you ever judge anyone? We are on our own paths, the ones God has laid out for our lives. That's all it is. We are no different. We are just taking the road before us, trying to get closer to our destination. We are trying to keep our ships afloat and sail to a safe port.

Remember that as you meet and greet the people who enter your life. Be the cool glass of water every weary traveler needs. Give comfort and love, not judgement and criticism.

With those thoughts of love and grace, I will show you how much I had to learn when it came to relationships. Please be gentle. I am a work in progress, and sometimes there was a lot of work to be done.

The Boy with the Giant Orange Bunny

My relationship troubles have been happening almost as long as I have been dating. I had my first boyfriend in the seventh grade, Bobby Williams. He would call me after school and play the song "Crimson and Clover" over and over. We listened to it for hours.

About the same time, a boy named Brad saw me in classes and in the halls of our school. He started talking to me, calling me, and asked me to "go steady," whatever that meant in the 1960s. He and his best friend walked to my house, which was quite a way from his, to bring me a giant orange bunny as a gift. I kept that bunny until I was in my twenties, even after Brad broke up with me to go steady with another girl.

In the ninth grade our paths crossed again. By then, Brad was an athlete, playing football and wrestling. I was in pep club and went to a lot of sporting events. Brad started talking to me again and asked me to go steady. I was enchanted with him and accepted. It lasted until he broke up with me to date another girl.

Then came high school, and the game changed.

Brad's journey led him to doing drugs with a girl. Our paths did not cross again for years. After we graduated in 1972, Brad married a freshman he was dating at the time, and on June 9, 1972, I married a senior I was dating.

I was eighteen years old, and, although I would like to say I married for love, that wasn't the case. I was looking for a calm port during a storm. I was looking for a way to escape my abusive stepfather, and the reality is that any port would have been better than the one I was anchored in. The parents of my first husband, who were both Pentecostal Holiness preachers, were kind and caring, and whenever I was with them, they made me feel like I was in a safe place.

They led a small church, and their sermons terrified me. I had never experienced people speaking in tongues, screaming, and rolling in the floor. The churches I had attended as a child were more mainstream, and we never saw anyone experience the Holy Spirit like that.

When I told my husband that I wasn't comfortable with his parents' church, he told me it was my duty to go. I needed to represent him and create the image that would allow him to stay home and smoke cigarettes. His parents did not know many of the things he was hiding from them. As an eighteen-year-old girl, I did what my husband told me to do. If he had asked me to be a chair, I would have gladly done so.

His parents helped us buy an 800-square-foot-home not far from them. The house had a one-car garage with a washer and dryer. After the washer broke down, we looked in the paper for a used one and found one for sale two blocks away. My husband and his best friend went over that Saturday to buy it and bring it home. They were in the garage hooking up the washer when I asked the name of the couple who sold it to us. My husband said their names, and it was all I could do to stay quiet. We had bought our washer from my junior high school boyfriend, Brad, who was living within two blocks of me.

I never said a thing to my husband. I never told him that I knew the man he bought our washer from, and not only did I know him, but he was my 7th grade and 9th grade boyfriend. It was my secret, one that I held close to my heart.

There's an adage about preachers' kids, a stereotype that says they grow up to be wild adults. I can't speak for anyone else, but I can say that my first husband didn't do anything to disprove those ideas. He spent a lot of time in Las Vegas with his friends gambling and doing things that had to stay in Vegas. That was no way to live as a married couple, and we divorced in 1976 when I was twenty-two, just four years after our wedding. I moved into my own apartment.

That should have come as no surprise. One of our problems was that we had married too young. On our wedding day, I was eighteen years old, and he was twenty-one. Neither one of us had the life skills or experience that we needed to make a marriage work.

Brad was also divorced by then and had started seeing another girl that he had dated in high school. By coincidence, or more accurately providence because there are no coincidences, that girl and I lived in the same apartment complex. She lived in one of the apartments on the back row, and I lived in one on the front row by the street. Brad was picking her up one night for a date, and as he drove out, she told him, "You know, I sometimes think I will see you picking Melanie Harding at her apartment. You have always said, 'Whoever married Melanie Harding got a really great person.'"

He must have taken that comment to heart. After that date he dropped her off, went straight home, and called my mother. He knew her phone number by heart, because when we were in junior high and going steady, he called me all the time. My mother lived at the same house and had the same phone number all those years later.

When he called, my mother answered her kitchen phone. Brad said who he was and asked if she could tell him how to reach me. She answered, "She's here laying on the couch in the living room. She's been sick."

After hearing that, he asked to speak to me, and my mom handed me the phone. He and I talked for a few minutes, and he told me he wanted to see me. I said that due to stress I was suffering from something close to a bleeding ulcer. The doctor told me to rest, and I could not be alone. That was why I was at my mother's house. I couldn't do much and didn't know if a date would be the best thing for me, regardless of how much I may have wanted to go.

He said he didn't care. He said we didn't need to do anything fancy. We could just go to a coffee shop, catch up, and visit for a while.

I agreed to meet him, and he picked me up the next evening. The sparks were instantaneous. It was as if we had never spent any time apart, like we were still in high school. It went so well that at the end of the date, he kissed me goodnight.

That night confirmed something I felt almost every time we were together: there was a special connection between us, one that made me feel like our souls were meant to be together. That flame had not died out, and on July 9th of that year we married. We were blissful and happy, and on October 16th of 1980 I gave birth to my son.

The first five years of our marriage were wonderful. We traveled, snow skied, hiked, ran together, bought a Hobie Cat sixteen-foot catamaran, and had fun all the time. We enjoyed each other's company, and the intimacy in our marriage was nothing I had ever experienced.

Everything was blissful until the company my husband was working for filed for bankruptcy and he was laid off in 1983. I wanted to keep being a stay-at-home mom, but we didn't have the money. My husband started his own electrical company to survive, and we did what we could to pay our bills.

Unfortunately, that was not enough.

After ten years, our relationship started down the road to destruction. Brad went back to the drugs and alcohol I thought he had left in his past. I did not like that world and did not want to be a part of it. His father was a violent alcoholic. I did not understand what that meant at the time or the damage alcoholism does to the children of people with drinking problems. I didn't understand the pull that alcohol and drugs can have on someone's soul.

My parents did not drink, and neither did my grandparents or any of my aunts and uncles. My parents might have had an occasional cold beer in the summer while grilling out, but that was it. The concept of substance abuse was foreign to me.

I did know that if we were visiting Brad's parents and his dad was drinking, I got scared. When the alcohol came out, screaming and yelling were sure to follow, and that frightened me. My parents never raised their voices. Hearing people argue triggered memories of my stepfather, but at that point I had not begun my journey to understand what all of that was about. If I had been more self-aware, maybe it would not have been such a challenge for me.

When Brad relapsed, he started pulling away from me and our young son. I tried everything I knew to stop our ship from sinking. The day he told me he needed me to drive him to the airport was the beginning of the end. He said he was flying to Colorado to go hiking, something the two of us had done many times. I asked him when he would be back. He said he did not know. He was going to go find himself. At the airport, he would not let me get out of the car to wait with him at the gate, which we could do in the days before the September 11th terror attacks. When Brad grabbed his backpack from the trunk and walked into the airport, he never looked back.

On May 15th, 1987, when I was thirty-three years old, we divorced. Losing that relationship broke me in two, and the pain and what I had to endure set me on a path of self-destruction that forced me into an inpatient treatment center.

Fear took over and I cratered. I believed that I could not breath without that man. I deeply loved him. I began spiraling out of control, falling apart.

During the process of unraveling our lives together, which was painful for me and our young son, I was standing at my stove stirring something and talking to God. "God, I want to kill myself," I said.

It wasn't just a few words in my kitchen. When I drove to work in the morning and saw a bridge or a concrete retaining wall, I thought, "If I hit that at a high speed, will it kill me and end this pain? I cannot live without Brad. I do not want to be single. God, I prayed to you to give me a son, and you answered my prayer. I will stay alive until he is eighteen years old. Then I will be done on Earth."

That may have been my plan, but it wasn't God's. Our God is cunning, baffling, and powerful, and He turned what I thought was the end of my life into a miracle.

Things got worse before they got better. In May of 1989, my son announced that he wanted to live with his father. I could not bear the pain and heartbreak I felt, and I spun out of control. The next few weeks were excruciating, and the fact that my son and husband were living without me in a house close to mine tore me to pieces. On May 15, 1989, I sold my house and moved to Saint Charles, Missouri in one weekend. I was thirty-five years old, and I had put myself on an island to avoid the trauma that had been forced on me.

After I put the pieces of my soul back together, I had the chance to visit with Brad. I needed to understand why he had treated me like he did, abandoning me at the airport and leaving me to raise our son by myself. He told me, "I didn't want to be married anymore, but I didn't have the courage to end it. I knew if I pushed you, you would get rid of me."

"Good job," I said. "Your plan worked."

Painful Lessons of the Heart

I had to do something to fill the hole that was created after my divorce from Brad, and I went back to my old ways, to a place that I thought would bring me peace and security. A man I had dated was living in Saint Charles, and once he found out I was there he contacted me. He made it clear that he wanted to marry me as soon as possible. It wasn't long before I had my Brittany Spears moment, and I agreed to tie the knot with him. In true rock star fashion, we flew to Vegas and said our vows at the Little White Chapel.

Not long after the heat cooled off, I started to see his true colors. I learned that he had been using illegal steroids to compete in body-building competitions. He became physically abusive, and in October of 1989 when I no longer felt safe, I moved back to Oklahoma City. On February 16th of 1990, three months after our wedding, our marriage was annulled.

Not long after, I was offered a position to help a doctor's clinic transition from handwritten statements and insurance billing to an accounting software system. My responsibilities included training his accounting employees. I accepted the position, and the doctor gave me a front office in his clinic. I began my research and selected a great medical software package. I chose one of his accounting staff to go with me to

Austin, Texas for the training. We went, came back, installed the new software, and trained the rest of the accounting department. It was a successful project, and it allowed angels into my life to further God's plan for my life.

I must have learned some things of the next few months, because on December 3rd of 1990, I checked myself in to an inpatient treatment center for thirty days to deal with my co-dependency issues. I put all of my energy into growing as a person and tried to take advantage of every opportunity that the treatment center gave me. But doing well in a treatment center is only a small part of the battle. The real work begins when you step outside that secluded environment and try to make your way in the real world. I may have learned a lot in the center, but it didn't take long for my past to catch up with me once I left.

I still felt a gap in my life that I needed to fill. I didn't think a man could do that for me, so I wanted to adopt a baby. Surely an infant would give me the validation and love I needed. I knew that a married couple would have a better chance of adopting a baby than a single woman, so I married again on March 3, 1991. I picked yet another winner. He looked great on the outside. He was well educated and a great conversationalist. But that was as far as things went. When I told him that I wanted to have children but couldn't, he found his way into my heart and played it for all it was worth.

The day after we married, my husband told me he was gay and that he had no intentions of living with me, despite what he had said. We never had sex and were only together as husband and wife for one day. By the time I was thirty-eight, on February 11, 1992, that marriage was annulled. To make it even more painful, I paid all the legal fees. It wasn't enough that I was choosing the wrong men left and right. I had upped the ante and was now draining my bank account when things fell apart. On March 4, 1992, I filed for bankruptcy in an attempt to start over, at least financially.

Blinded by what I thought would be a fresh start, I fell back into my old patterns. On August 21, 1992, I thought I had found true love and married again. It didn't seem like I had learned anything, and this time I wed a recovering alcoholic and heroin addict with two sons. The three of them moved into my house, and the terror began.

I discovered that my stepsons were both violent drug users who punched holes in my walls. When they were not filling pillowcases with baseballs and beating my son with them, they were stealing my jewelry, selling it on the playground, and using the money to buy drugs.

That was a breaking point for me. I had put myself in painful situations, but I had never allowed anyone to harm my child. I separated from my husband on May 1st, 1993 and began working with my sponsor and a therapist to heal whatever wounds were causing me to fall into such terrible relationships.

I put my blinders on and ignored anything that didn't help me heal. I was single for eleven years, focused only on becoming the person God wants me to be.

That could have been my happy ending. I could have spent the rest of my life working on me, growing into the happy, healthy person I needed to be.

In a moment of weakness, I listened to the small voice inside me that wanted me to turn back to my old ways, the voice that I could never silence. It told me I was tired, and that I deserved an easy life. The voice said I could have one now, if I found the right man. And then someone came into my life and promised all of those things.

Teatime With an Angel

The doctor who hired me to help with his software thought about purchasing a larger home and put down a $5,000 check to hold the property for him. He changed his mind and asked that I meet the real estate agent for lunch and get his check back.

I went to the meeting, which was at a restaurant close to his clinic. The agent returned the doctor's check with no problem. She and I began to visit over glasses of iced tea, but not long into our conversation she stopped me and said, "I cannot sit here with you anymore. You are making me crazy." She was picking up on all the negative energy in my life.

She must have sensed I needed serious help. What she couldn't have known was that I was carrying a loaded gun underneath the seat of my car. Despite my promise to stay alive until my son turned eighteen, I carried a pistol with me in case my pain became too much for me to bear. I was telling God I would stay here if I could, and I was trying with all my might to hold on, but my pain was unbearable. When I was driving, I often thought, "I could pull over behind that bridge and end this." But I stayed true to my promise and kept the gun under my seat instead of turning it on myself.

The real estate agent told me if I wanted help there was a women's group that met on Wednesday nights at a place called Chance to Change. I felt a strong pull to attend the meeting, but I didn't know why. It was the Holy Spirit, my intuition, reaching out to save me.

I walked through the door at Chance to Change not long after my conversation with the angel who was holding a check for my boss. I felt peace knowing that I was supposed to be there. There were seven women at the meeting, including one who was the facilitator. They were sitting on pillows on the floor, and I took a pillow and listened. Weeks passed. I went and listened but did not speak. I just felt the energy in the room to see if it was a safe place. No one had to pay a single cent to go there. To this day, I do not know how the organization was funded.

One night I noticed one of the regulars, a young woman, was missing. I knew she was a law student at the University of Oklahoma, but that was about it. I asked about her and was told she would be gone for a while.

Time went on. I continued to be drawn to the comfort of those meetings, to the understanding of those women. I did not know them well, but there was a common thread that somehow connected us.

One Wednesday, the law student returned. She looked different, refreshed, enlightened. Her complexion was glowing. Peace and happiness radiated in her smile and laughter.

She did not look like this when she had attended meetings before, and questions raced through my mind. "Where had she been? What drug did she take? What had given her this peaceful, happy state of mind?"

The facilitator asked me to take a test. I had to answer questions like, "Is the sky blue? What color are clouds?" They were obscure questions, ones that don't seem to have any correct answers. I will not go into the details, but let's say that I failed the test.

When it was almost Christmas, the facilitator of the group called me at work, and we met about my test results. She gave me two choices. "Do you want to spend Christmas in cold weather or warm weather?"

"I want to go where that law student went," I said.

They flew me non-stop to Sierra Tucson, an inpatient treatment center in Arizona. I had no money, and my insurance would not cover this cost, but that didn't matter. Somehow, the organization was able to pay for everything. I do not know who purchased my airline ticket. I have no idea who paid the $25,000 for my month of treatment. All that I know is that God sent angels to surround me when I was broken to the core. I was grateful for the opportunity to heal but I also felt embarrassed that people I loved were able to break me. How could that be? Why did I need to be treated in the first place? Why had I agreed to be close to people who wanted to destroy me?

God knew I had caused myself pain because of the choices I made. He also had a solution. People showed up in my life with the right help at the right time. They were proof that God is powerful, that He loves us, and that He is always watching our path, which is beyond comprehension.

I experienced one of the most incredible Christmases I have ever had in my life at Sierra Tucson. I arrived at there the first day of December and wouldn't leave until after New Year's. We gathered in a large dining hall that backed up to the mountains and saw stars twinkling through large windows. Someone was playing Christmas music on a baby grand piano. The awe I experienced was the same feeling I had when I was a small child on my grandparents' farm.

A huge Christmas tree was decorated with thousands of twinkling lights. I looked underneath the tree and saw hundreds of large teddy bears of different colors with big red bows around their necks. The staff greeted us. We sang songs together. We prayed. Then they said to us, "Go pick out a teddy bear. It's your present." I still have my bear.

I spent a month with the most amazing people and powerful teachers. The facility celebrated when a patient had completed their treatment and was leaving. After their last dinner at the facility, the other patients formed a huge circle holding hands. The person leaving stood in the middle while the others sang "The Rose," which had been made famous by Bette Midler.

As we sang each verse, tears fell down on the checks of the person leaving. They were not tears of sadness, but joy. They had made it. They had completed the first thirty days of their recovery and had the tools to go back into the world and live a happy peaceful life.

The last paragraph of the song was particularly powerful. It goes like this:

> *When the night has been too lonely*
> *And the road has been too long*
> *And you think that love is only*
> *For the lucky and the strong*
> *Just remember in the winter*
> *Far beneath the bitter snows*
> *Lies the seed that with the sun's love*
> *In the spring becomes the rose.*

Each time I sang that song for someone else, I thought, "Someday I will be standing in that circle, and they will be singing to me."

An important part of my time at the inpatient facility was Family Week. The idea was that when patients were close to being released, their families would come to the center and applaud them for the hard work they had put into becoming better people.

I believed my mother and sister would come to Arizona for my family week so we could heal together and be the loving close family we used to be, or at least the one I thought we had been. My facilitator Sal talked to my family three times, and I looked forward to them being there.

My hopes were shattered when only my son showed up. My son and I went through that week together, and I later found out why he was the only family member who came. My mother told Sal, a big, tall Italian man, that she didn't show up as a way of punishing me for sharing our family secrets with strangers. Sal was able to take the pain and rejection I felt and transform it into a lesson. "When people show you who they are," he said, "believe them."

I don't know what my mother was thinking when she thought she had to punish me. Sharing my pain with relative strangers was punishment enough. To share the truth, my truth, was not pretty. It is not roses and beautiful music. It is not Ward and June Cleaver and the Beaver, as much as I thought that it would be.

Revealing your wounds in public is terrible, horrific, and beyond what any one human being should have to experience. But it's what you have to do to grow, and that has been part of God's perfect plan for my life. He gave me the strength to endure, grow, and learn through all of it, and I would rather be punished by my family than stay the person I was.

Before I could leave the safety and serenity of the center, I had to meet with Sal, who really understood me. He was a wonderful person, and my life is better because of the time I spent with him.

Sal spoke with me about many things I would face when I left the facility. He told me that 10 percent of my work was in the treatment center and the other 90 percent would happen in the real world. I had only completed 10 percent and knew how hard that had been. How would I be able to handle the other 90 percent when I got home and was all by myself?

Sal added another challenge to my recovery. He told me that in his twenty years of practice, he had never talked to a sicker family than mine. I will never forget what he said next. "Melanie, if you are going to stay alive, you have to divorce your family."

What? How does someone do that? At that time in my life, I could not comprehend what that meant or how anyone could do that. I loved my family, despite how flawed they were and how painful it was when we were together.

We were each given a daily reading meditation book. I carried it with me all the time. Sal took my book, and he said "Melanie, I don't usually do this, but I know your pink cloud is going to be a hard fall. When it does, call me at this number." He wrote his number in my journal and told me that I would arrive home under a pink cloud, meaning that everything would be safe and warm, but within a few weeks that pink cloud would burst. He was a wise man. I came back home, and before long, the cloud was gone. I called Sal, just like he told me to.

He told me I needed to wait for God's timing, that things would happen when they were supposed to happen. Waiting was hard. I get impatient. It is hard for me to understand that my twenty-four-hour day is not a twenty-four-hour day in God's time.

The next several years I focused on my therapy and worked on myself so that I could stop being the codependent woman my mother had taught me to be. That mindset had turned me into the kind of adult who did what you wanted her to do. If you wanted me to become a chair, I became one. My sense of self was gone. I lost it somewhere along the way. During that time, I just wanted to be loved and to have a family. I would do whatever the people around me wanted me to do because I thought was the only way I could find love. I became the person they said they needed me to be, not the one that was part of God's plan.

In 1994, I was going through the pain of another relationship ending. I was on the floor of my bedroom sobbing my eyes out. It was one of those deep cries where you cannot breathe, from the kind of pain that is rooted in desperation.

I started talking to God. I said, "Dear God, I cannot handle this pain anymore. I do not know what to do. I want to be so close to you that I can lay my head on your lap and rest. I'm so tired. I'll do whatever that takes."

But, as they say, "Be careful what you pray for, you just might get it."

I think of a verse in Luke 10: 25-28. Jesus is with His disciples, and other people are there. A lawyer stood up and tested Him. The lawyer asked, "Teacher, what shall I do to inherit eternal life?"

Jesus asked the lawyer, "What do you think? What have you read in the law about eternal life?"

The lawyer answered, "You shall love the Lord your God with all your heart, with all your soul, with all your strength, and with all your might and love your neighbor as yourself."

Then Jesus said to the lawyer, "That is the answer. Do this and you will have eternal life." Jesus was telling all of us, "Love me. Come home."

This was the peace I wanted. I wanted to love God and to return home to Him.

Best Breakup Ever

I t took years for me to fully learn the lessons that had been taught to me in Sierra Tucson. When Sal told me that I was going to have to divorce my family if I was going to make it and stay alive, he wasn't just talking about my relatives. Working on yourself may mean that you no longer connect with people in your life who aren't willing to grow, and that's okay. Sal told me that the life I would have without them would be much better than the one I would have if things stayed the same.

Sal understood I couldn't be around my family because I feared them, and I wasn't strong enough to deal with them. I had healed just enough to keep my head above water at that point, and if there was any rough water, I might be swept away and struggle to stay afloat.

I told Sal there was no way I could cut my family out of my life. I felt the bonds between me and my family were too strong. Fortunately, I didn't have to make the choice. When I returned home, I tried to connect with them and attempted to bring us together. The more I did that, the further they ran from me.

After I returned from Sierra Tucson, my mother had open heart surgery and I was her caregiver. I lived nearby and was still trying to turn the family I had been given into the one I wanted. My sister never came home to help me care for our mother, which became a problem when my mother suffered complications. Her legs got a staph infection at the site where the doctors removed veins from her legs to transplant in her heart. A nurse taught me how to change my mother's dressing and take care of her wounds. Each morning, every day during lunch time, and after work I went to my mother's house and changed her dressing. I cooked her meals and spent the night with her when she was scared. I did my best to be a good daughter and didn't worry about how much time or energy it cost me.

Fortunately, I had the most amazing boss. He understood the situation. He was forgiving when I had to feed my mother lunch, which took over an hour. For his kindness I remain forever grateful. I was struggling, and I think he saw it. He was an angel who gave me the time and freedom to do the things I need to do.

Despite my hard work, my mother's condition worsened, and I had to take her back to the hospital. She was frightened and did not want to stay overnight by herself. I had to go to work and take care of my son, and staying at the hospital would have been difficult, but I didn't want my mother to be alone. I called my sister in California and was able to convince her to fly to Oklahoma, go to the hospital, and spend the night in our mother's hospital room on a cot so that our mother would not be alone and afraid. My sister agreed and flew out to visit our mother in the hospital, but she did not stay with her. My sister and her son spent the night in our mother's house.

When our mother was released, she called me on the phone. She said she and my sister would like for me to come over for breakfast before I went to work. I wanted to go but I didn't have the time. My boss had been so kind to me by allowing me to take time off to care for my mother, and I did not want to be late for work yet again. I hate to admit this, but I called him and told a white lie. I said I had an early dentist appointment, and I would be a little late getting to work.

I drive to my mother's house expecting to have breakfast with my family. When I pulled up to my mother's house there was an unfamiliar car parked in front of it. The street my mother lived on was full of homes that had one-car garages, so it was not unusual for cars to be parked on the street. I didn't think much of it.

When I walked to the door, my mother was sitting in her recliner at the end of the living room. To the right of my mother sat a man that I did not recognize. My sister was sitting on my mother's left in a brown rocking chair. Directly in front of my mother's recliner was a chair where my mother asked me to sit.

I sat, and my mother told me that she and my sister had been up all night making decisions. She introduced the man on the couch as her personal attorney.

My mother asked me to sign papers that her attorney had with him. She explained that she no longer wanted to be my mother. My mother wanted my sister to be recognized as her only child. Signing the papers meant that I would give up any rights I had as her daughter.

"Breathe through the pain and shock," I told myself as the three of them stared at me. I calmed my breathing and asked my mother, "Is this what you want?"

She said, "Yes, it is."

I said, "I'm going to ask you again. Is this what you really want?"

She said, "Yes, it is."

"I am going to ask you for the third time. Will this make you happy?"

"Yes."

"I want you to be happy," I said. "I will never cause you any problem. I will never go to court and tell them I am your daughter. I love both of you so very much and I want you both to be happy."

I turned to her attorney and said, "I will never sign any legal document. I will never show up or cause her or my sister any problems. Do not waste my mother's money by sending me legal documents to sign."

I stood up and again told my mother and sister how much I loved them, that I hoped they would be happy, and that I had to leave because I was late for work.

I never saw either of them again. The decision to be apart was not mine. I would have loved to have healed the wounds that had torn our family apart, but I was never given the chance.

My mother's attorney called me the next day at work. "I am so sorry," he said. "Your mother did not tell me that you did not know what was going to happen."

He was right. I had been blindsided, and I sensed he had been, too. I told him he was innocent because he had no idea of our family history or why my mother had allowed that to happen.

"If I had four children and it was the end of my life and I only had four pennies to my name," he said, "I would leave one penny to each of my children. And I would want the four of them to decide together as a family if there was a need to cut off my life support." It was his way of saying that he couldn't comprehend why my mother had done what she had done.

"I would do whatever I could for my family during at the end of my life to show them how much I loved them," he continued. He apologized to me profusely before we hung up.

I never heard from him again, but at least one positive thing came out of that call. I had an honest connection with another human being. Someone had witnessed my suffering and offered me genuine concern, a moment of unconditional love that my mother and sister had never been able to give me. Even though we didn't know each other, that attorney and I were able to lower our walls and bond over the importance of family and the injustice of what my family had done.

After I got off the call, I felt the grief that appears whenever you lose a relationship. After a while, and after I had the chance to talk about the event with someone close to me, it dawned on me that my family had done me a favor and had given me a great gift. Because they made the hurtful decision to cut me out of their lives, I did not have to go through the pain and agony of divorcing them. They had taken the decision out of my hands and done the hurtful work for me. I did not have to do anything other than heal and work on myself. My family had given me my freedom, the liberty that I desperately needed even though I had not known it was a possibility. God stepped in to take care of me, and He had arranged it so that I had to do nothing but accept what had happened and move forward.

It wasn't easy, but I finally let go and let my sister and mother live on their terms. I honored my word and made no attempt to be a part of their lives. I never contacted my mother, and after she passed away, I made no effort to collect from her estate. As far as I know, my sister and her second husband live in California.

Years after my meeting with my mother and her attorney, my son approached me and told me that my mother was dying. "Did she ask to see me?" I asked.

"No," my son replied.

"Then I can't visit her," I told him. "I gave them my word." It was tragic, but there was no sense in me going to a place where I wasn't wanted and where my presence would serve no purpose other than to cause strife. It became even more tragic when my mother passed away shortly after my son told me about her sickness.

My son didn't understand why I couldn't go to the hospital or the funeral, but the only way for me to honor my word and respect the choice my mother had made years before was to stay away. If I am not as good as my word, what am I? My son was so upset with me that we didn't speak for weeks, and when he did talk to me, he told me how angry he was that I hadn't gone to my mother's funeral.

I have wondered if my mother was looking for her freedom when she asked me to sign that document. Maybe she thought that my signature on that document would give her peace and absolve her from the choices she had made about me and our relationship. Perhaps it was her way of alleviating a lot of her pain.

I learned that we can't chose what family we are born into, but throughout our lives, God replaces some of those people with his angels.

Another lesson that I learned was that God never gave up on me. He kept putting chosen people on my path. Those angels taught me and helped me heal a little bit at a time when I was ready for the next level of understanding and healing. Without them, I never would have accepted the divorce from my family as a gift.

Tuxedo Man

Nine years after I left Sierra Tucson, I was forty-nine years old, working, raising my son, and in therapy focusing on healing and learning about me. I thought I had recovered from all the insanity of my past. I believed I could not be tricked or become weak about who I was as a person.

I learned there are levels to wellness. Healing takes time and growth, and it has turns and weaves back and forth over mountains and thru deep valleys. Getting into a real relationship with God is a journey. I was not there yet, even though I thought I was.

I had been single for those nine years, and a single mother at that. For more than eight years, I had a job I enjoyed in upper management of a Fortune 500 company.

I had spent the previous fourteen years working hard. At times, I held two or three jobs at a time. I had relationships that proved to be some of my greatest teachers and areas of growth during those years, but they had all ended painfully. I was tired, so tired, and I wasn't reading my Bible or spending time with God like I should have been. That's how you lose your life. Sheep don't get lost on purpose. They take a few steps away from the flock, start eating, and before they know it, they are miles away from the rest of the group.

The Beginning of Salvation--
The Word

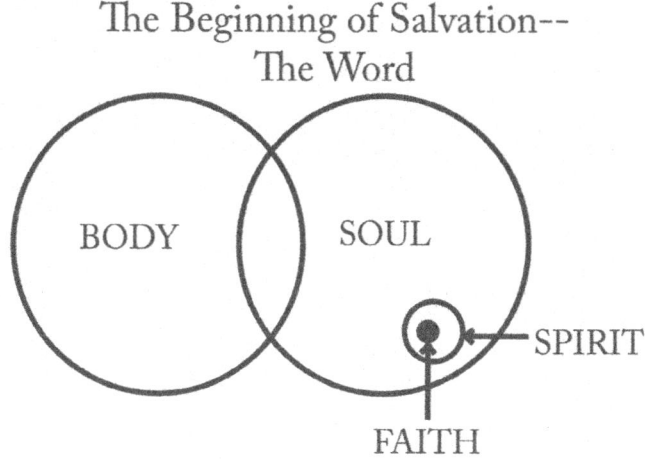

BODY   SOUL

SPIRIT

FAITH

Failing to keep a spiritual connection, the tether between me and God, was a slippery slope. Satan was watching me and said to himself, "Perfect timing. I will get her to cross over to my side. I know exactly what I will send her way that will take her to the bottom. Then she will give up and lose her faith in God."

According to Jesus, Satan comes to do three things. He wants to kill, steal, and destroy us. People who seem so nice while you are sharing lunch with them can be the tools that Satan uses to kill, steal, and destroy you. Remember this truth when you are praying to God: Satan is listening. Satan will dress up an individual or a situation to look exactly like what he heard you ask God for.

Satan knows what he is doing, and he knows you well. He knew my desire, the one flaw he could exploit the most, was my need to be loved. I yearned to have a family, to live a comfortable life, and to not have to work. I craved someone who would love me and want to walk through life with me. Satan even heard me when I told God (I said this out loud standing in my kitchen and was this specific) that I was giving up "Melanie's plan," that I was handing my life over to God. I told God that if He ever wanted me to be married again, He would have to send the man to my front door wearing a tuxedo and holding red roses. Satan heard every single word I said and was waiting for the right time to spring his trap on me.

A man saw me at a business after-hours get-together. I had been invited to a lot of those, but I had never gone to one before. I was talking to a group of people I worked with when the man walked into the circle, introduced himself, and asked where everyone worked. I just listened. I did not say my name. I only said that we all worked at the same large corporation that provided pharmaceuticals to assisted living and nursing home facilities.

The next morning, the man started calling assisted living facilities in the city. He said he was considering buying a facility and wanted to know which company provided medications to the patients who lived at their facility. The manager gave him the name and number of the company where I worked, and the man called it.

Everyone knew me in the office, especially the receptionist. The man asked if someone with my description worked there. She said yes and put him through to my phone. I picked up my phone and, bingo, I was talking to him.

The man invited me to lunch, and I met him at a restaurant that was halfway between our two offices. He seemed nice and was a high-level engineer in one of the largest oil and gas companies in the city. He shared with me where he went to college, his business career, and all the places around the world he had traveled for work.

As I was saying good-bye, he said he was leaving town the next weekend. He did not want to wait until he got back to take me to dinner and asked if I would have lunch with him the Friday before he left. I accepted.

That is when his "full court press" began.

The next thing I knew, this man, whom I had only known for a short time, showed up in a tuxedo, holding red roses and a bottle of wine. Tuxedo Man, as I now call him, wanted to take me to the annual Renaissance Ball at the Oklahoma City Golf & Country Club on our second date. I slid down that slippery slope as fast as I could.

It seemed as if my prayers had been answered. Not long before this, I told God that if he wanted me to be in a relationship, I needed to see a man at my door in a tuxedo with roses and a bottle of wine. When, Tuxedo Man appeared on my doorstep, I thought the only explanation was an answer to prayer.

I let down my guard, and in the blink of an eye, I went from emotion right into will, blowing past reason. God was watching this unfold, knowing that this was the one last lesson I needed to get back on His plan for my life.

Tuxedo Man and I dated for about two months. In that time, he wanted me to see all the property he owned. It was important to him that I understood he was wealthy. We flew to Iowa, where he owned two buildings on The University of Iowa campus. One had a convenience store in it. The other one housed a printing business.

We walked around campus and Tuxedo Man showed me the fraternity house he had lived in and the buildings where he had taken classes. He took me to the house where he grew up with his younger brother, a nice two-story brick home on a corner.

His parents had passed away before I met him, but I learned his father was an educator. His mother was a writer and journalist for the local paper. Both of his parents were serious golfers, and his mother was on the Board of Directors for the Iowa Golf Association.

When his parents died, the properties they had acquired during their lifetimes were divided between Tuxedo Man and his brother. The two buildings on the Iowa campus were his inheritance. The next weekend we flew to Jackson Hole, Wyoming and stayed at a five-star hotel in the middle of town. We went snow skiing up in the mountains and ate dinner at a marvelous restaurant, The Snake River Grill.

I was in an element I really enjoyed, which was what Tuxedo Man wanted. He wanted me to be drawn into his riches so that I would let my guard down. It's easier to catch your prey when they don't think you are a threat.

We flew to Minneapolis, Minnesota and stayed at another five-star hotel. Tuxedo Man told me to bring a black dress, one fit for formal events. He had bought tickets for us to go to *The Phantom of the Opera* with the original cast from London performing.

He rented a car at the airport, and the day after seeing the play we drove out of town. He said we were going to his "lake house" on Ten Mile Lake in Walker, Minnesota. He made sure to describe the private sandy beach and boat dock. Are you getting the picture now? He was showing me all of his worldly possessions, and implying this easy, carefree life could be mine if I would push God's plan to the side.

It was a beautiful drive through lovely small towns full of gorgeous huge trees. We arrived at the lake house which had been left to him and his brother. His brother raced dogs in the Iditarod race in Alaska, and that seemed to be where he spent most of his time and energy.

Tuxedo Man's brother and his wife had no desire to be there, so Tuxedo Man almost always had it to himself. It was a lovely large log cabin with an additional log home on the back, a guest cottage that slept eight. After seeing that, I was in awe, and I wanted this life to be mine. I had taken the shiny bait and swallowed the platinum hook, which was exactly his intention.

I am sharing these facts not to justify my actions, but to admit that I was overwhelmed with the "easy beautiful life" that was being presented to me on a silver platter.

I had let myself get physically and mentally exhausted after working hard from the time I was sixteen years old and began making decisions from my human self, my self-will. At that moment I closed the door between me and my relationship with God and unplugged my extension cord from divine guidance. And that made it easy for Satan to come through the door carrying roses and wine.

Tuxedo Man told me we could travel and that I wouldn't have to work again. It seemed like an answer to prayer. I allowed myself to be enticed and allured by his promises, which turned out to be lies. He convinced me to quit a wonderful job and career and to sell my home, my furniture, everything I owned. He said we were going to start all over and would buy everything new.

I agreed with him and sold all the things I thought I would no longer need. That left me with almost nothing. I had no equity in the home I had bought on a lease-purchase agreement, and the fees I incurred after selling the house meant I owed money on the deal. My belongings had been sold at fire-sale prices in a garage sale, and I made nothing from that.

It sounded and felt like love to me, so giving up all of my possessions was not an issue. As far as I was concerned, it was an act of love. Besides, Tuxedo Man was my one true love, and I didn't need those things. He was going to take care of me forever. We married on March 14, 2004, in a small Episcopalian church in Jackson Hole, Wyoming, a dreamlike beginning to another nightmare.

It didn't take long for the wheels to fall off my Cinderella carriage. Not long after our wedding, I needed a place in our house for an office, so I painted an empty bedroom and made a makeshift desk out of boxes and wood.

When Tuxedo Man came home, he asked, "What do you think you are doing? You didn't ask for permission." He put a long desk in front of his, a place for me to work where he could watch everything I did.

It came time for the Prix de West, an annual auction at the National Cowboy & Western Heritage Museum in Oklahoma City. I had never been to the auction, but I learned that it attracts artists from all over the world. Tuxedo Man's daughter was home from college in Dallas, and the three of us attended. As we entered, we were each given ten tickets, which were to be used to bid on pieces of art.

I had just celebrated my fiftieth birthday, and Tuxedo Man offered me a generous gift. "Melanie, as a birthday present," he said, "you can buy whatever piece of art you want, up to $5,000." I was pleased that my new husband was being so generous.

We looked at every piece of art for sale, and I fell in love with one called "Lady in Red" by Patricia Dobson. It featured a traditional Native American pot draped in a red blanket. The pot sat on a table covered in a blue tablecloth, and in front of the pot was a bracelet. The painting spoke to me, and, interestingly, the song "Lady in Red" was one of my favorites. It was priced at $4,200, well within the budget Tuxedo Man had given me. To increase the chance that we would have the winning bid, he suggested all three of us place one ticket in the envelope. That way, I would have three chances to win instead of one.

When the bidding ended, I was thrilled to see that my ticket had been selected as the winner. The painting would be mine, and I looked forward to hanging it in our home. Tuxedo Man paid for it within the fifteen-minute window the auction allowed, but we wouldn't be able to take it home that night. All of the artwork had to remain in the museum until the end of September so that the public could view the great works of art that had been part of the auction. As a consolation, I was able to have my picture taken next to the painting, my face beaming with the knowledge I would be able to view this work of art every day for the rest of my life.

We met with the artist, Patricia, who liked meeting the people who purchased her work. She had spent nearly a year working on the painting, and it felt like a child to her. She wanted to make sure it wound up in a good home. I told her it was a birthday present from Tuxedo Man, and she seemed excited.

Not long after that, we spent a few weeks at Tuxedo Man's lake house in Minnesota before heading to Tucson, where he interviewed with a company about a job dredging canals in Africa. Ships carry bauxite from African mines to ports all around the world, where it is sent to companies who use it to manufacture aluminum, and it's important to keep the canals clear. The job carried a lot of responsibility, and I was happy for Tuxedo Man when he was hired.

The best part of the offer: the company's headquarters were in Paris, France, a place I had dreamed of visiting my entire life. When Tuxedo Man asked me if I wanted to live there for a few months, my answer was an enthusiastic, "Yes." Tuxedo Man assured me we would be home in time to pick up my painting in September.

My time in Paris started out blissfully. During the day, while Tuxedo Man was at work, I enjoyed some of the most stunning art in the world, attended the Cordon Bleu cooking school for a dessert class, and admired the fashion of Paris.

We stayed at a wonderful hotel one block from the Arc de Triomphe. Four days after I arrived, Tuxedo Man made dinner reservations for us, and the meal was enjoyable. How could it not be in Paris? Meals in France are slow, quiet, and relaxing, experiences that you can't rush.

I did not expect what Tuxedo Man had planned next. A car took us to an upscale theater house. The staff recognized him when we walked in and showed us to the best seats in the house. Drinks were delivered. It was clear this had been set up previously.

The lights dimmed and music started as the curtain went up. Hundreds of white pearl beads on strings descended from the ceiling as the music played. When a group of naked, beautiful, and tall French women danced within the pearl beads, I knew I was in trouble. Tuxedo Man had never shown me this side of his personality. He may have liked it, but it made me uncomfortable. If I had known it was going to happen, I might have been able to prepare myself, but because I didn't have any warning my only thought was, "How am I going to get out of here?"

Other than my discomfort at watching a group of naked women dance, the evening was calm and peaceful, especially the meal we shared.

The rest of the night was anything but tranquil. When we returned to the hotel, I witnessed something I had never seen before: a rage event. It was the most terrifying episode imaginable, like a valve being opened and releasing hate and anger that had been bottled up for years, a hate that had to attach itself to anyone who was close. It made me fear for my life and wonder if I had eaten my last meal. To make it even more terrifying, I was in a foreign country and did not know anyone who could help me.

Tuxedo Man started screaming and threw all my clothes out of the closet, including my hot rollers and makeup. He took my passport, grabbed my credit cards and all the cash I had in my purse, and hid my cell phone. Having that anger and negative energy directed at me was almost more than I could bear.

I tried to escape by jumping into a cab and rushing to the airport. I thought I could tell the ticket agent what was happening, and they would get me on the first flight to the U.S. But Tuxedo Man had taken my credit card, and I had no way to pay for a ticket. I thought the airline might understand the terror I was going through and find a way to send me home. The biggest obstacle was that I didn't have my passport, and there was nothing anyone could do about that, regardless of how good the airline's intentions may have been. It never occurred to me that I could have gone to the U.S. Embassy and gotten an emergency passport. Had I known that I would have visited the embassy and done whatever I could to leave the country.

Once I realized I couldn't leave France, I had a smaller and more practical problem to resolve. The cab driver needed to be paid, but I had no money. Thinking fast, I told the cab driver that my husband called me and told me to come back to hotel because he wanted to go to the airport, too. It was a bit of a stretch, but it worked. The driver turned around, and we went back to the scene of the crime.

When we arrived, the cab driver followed me into the hotel lobby. I asked the front desk for help and was able to get the money to pay the driver.

Over the next few days, I cried many tears and was terrified that I would be killed. I didn't know what Tuxedo Man was capable of and watching him fly into unprovoked rage made it clear he wasn't the man I thought he was. I slept in my clothes every night and waited until he left for work every morning. When he began to leave the day after he had his first rage event, I asked him, "How am I going to buy breakfast and lunch or even a Diet Coke? You have taken everything from me."

"There is a free breakfast downstairs if you wake up early enough. Other than that, you will eat with me when I come back at the end of the day," he said. With that, he walked away and left me on my own with no way to care for myself.

I did everything I could to distance myself from Tuxedo Man. I wore my headphones and listened to music twenty-four hours a day, knowing that this would keep me from having to talk to him.

We ate dinner together, but there was no conversation. One night, he tried to push my buttons by asking me questions and saying things he knew I didn't like. "This is all your fault," he told me. "You are not behaving the way a wife should."

I didn't take the bait and stayed silent. "I bet you don't even have a college degree," he continued.

When I had enough, I looked him in the eye. "You need to be quiet," I said. "If you say one more thing, I am going to stand up and scream. I don't care what these people think." I knew that he could not tolerate me causing a scene in a fancy restaurant and having people look at us like we were crazy. That was enough to make him stay quiet for the rest of the night.

When he left in the morning, I sat on the floor of our room with my belongings strewn about, sobbing my eyes out, terrified. What was I going to do? How was I going to get back to Oklahoma? I had locked myself in a velvet prison and had given the key to someone else.

Visiting Paris had been a dream of mine, and I jumped in with both feet when I was given the chance. That was part of the problem. Satan dresses up temptations to look wonderful on the outside, when they are full of danger on the inside. This is why it is so important to open the door between your spirit and your soul. It will keep you on God's path.

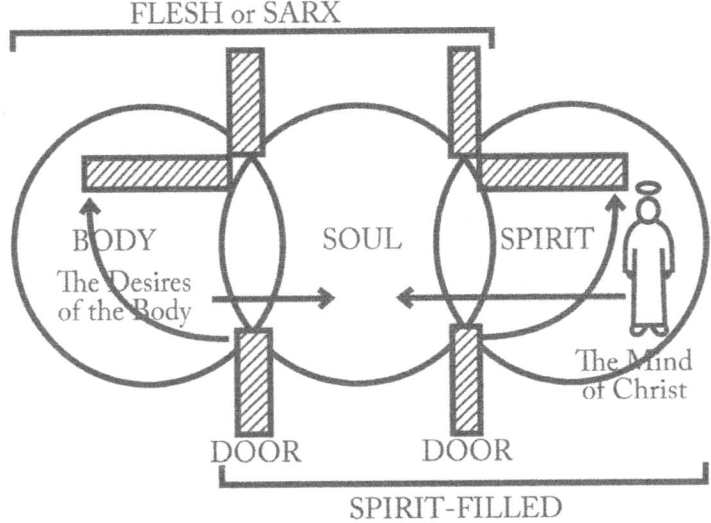

I used to be skeptical when I heard pastors teach about the Holy Spirit. That was until Pastor Harris became not only my pastor but also my teacher and spiritual mentor. He came into my life at the right moment. One day during worship service he asked the congregation, "Do you know what the Holy Spirit is?"

"It is our intuition," he explained.

That made sense to me. Think about the times you were going to do something, say something, or buy something. Your will says, "Yep, sounds good to me. I'm doing it."

Then you hear a voice inside of yourself, sometimes it is so strong you can feel it. Your intuition whispers, "No, this is not what I should be doing. It's not right for me." When we ignore that, we slide down a slippery slope, and are back in the same trouble we were before.

Here's what I learned after I let Tuxedo Man into my life even though I didn't know him well: If you don't know someone it is foolish to trust them. It seems silly that I didn't understand this before I was held hostage in a hotel in Paris. The idea had never crossed my mind, or, if it had, I wasn't able to hear it.

I learned to ask two questions when I met new people. The first is, "Do you trust them enough to know they have your best interest at heart?"

The second question is, "Do you trust them enough to make decisions for your life?"

I did not know to ask those two questions before I got involved with Tuxedo Man. I didn't even know these were good questions to ask.

I paid a high price for my ignorance.

Fortunately, God came to my rescue again in the form of a beautiful angel.

My Angel in Paris

As I sat on the floor of our hotel room terrified and not knowing how I was going to move past this, I heard a knock on the door. I opened it and saw a woman. Her name was Patty, and she was in Paris with her husband, who was working on the same project as Tuxedo Man for the same large American corporation.

She looked at me and at all my belongings thrown on the floor. Our eyes met. Her understanding, her grace, her support radiated through me. I told her what had happened and that I was trapped. I said that I could not get home to America and that I didn't know how I would eat for the next ten days.

I will never forget what she said or how it felt when I heard her say it. "Don't worry. I will feed you. You can spend each day with me." For the next ten days, she came to my room to pick me up after our husbands left for work. This had been their third two-week stint on the project, and she was familiar with Paris and how to maneuver the city's subway system.

She and her husband were staying on the same floor of the hotel as Tuxedo Man and I were. Each day she bought my breakfast, my lunch, and even a Diet Coke if I wanted one. We passed the days going to museums and wandering the streets of Paris.

We stopped at sidewalk cafés to sip coffee and talk. She told me that her husband had worked on projects with Tuxedo Man, and everyone knew he was violent, held rage deep within him, and was someone to stay away from. I wished someone had told me that before I was blinded by the houses and wealth he used to trap me.

When we weren't walking the placid and picturesque streets of Paris, I was able to stay in the living area of Patty's suite until Tuxedo Man returned at the end of the day. Then I had to go to dinner with him so that I could eat. After that, it was time for bed.

I needed Patty's company and comfort, and I would have stayed with her twenty-four hours a day if I could have, but I did not want to intrude on her and her husband's nightly dinner plans. Her husband was incredibly supportive. He told me he was sorry that I was treated so cruelly and warned me to be careful because Tuxedo Man was dangerous and could be ruthless.

On my last day in Paris, Patty, the angel sent by God, and I spent the day walking the streets, going from one small Paris café to another. We found ourselves at what had become her favorite café for afternoon coffee.

Our emotions were in the air, raw and pure. We had shared many things about ourselves during that week. There was a bond, a connection between us, that could only have been built by the Hand of the Almighty. Although we had only met a few days before, we had many things in common and had become close.

We told each other about our families and about the things that we would like to change if we had the power. One of hers was that she and her daughter were estranged. One of mine was that my mother did not care for me at all. My mother disliked me so much that she had written me a "hate letter" and instructed my sister to mail it to me after our mother passed away.

The letter had arrived in my mailbox, and I knew it was from my mother because I instantly recognized the beautiful cursive on the front of the envelope. I also knew it could be a time bomb, full of hate and anger, and I rushed over to see my therapist at the time, Dr. Cone.

"I have a bit of an emergency," I told him. By chance, someone had cancelled an appointment, and Dr. Cone ushered me in. I asked him to open the letter and read it. "If it's good, let me know and I will read it. If it's bad, I don't want to read it. I am not in a position to deal with any negative energy right now," I said.

"She says you were a good baby and did a good job rising your son," Dr. Cone said after he looked at the letter. "That's a good start."

He scanned the rest of the letter and paused. "Melanie, you don't need to read this," he said. "The person who wrote this is mentally ill." I followed him as he took a brass plate from his office and carried it out to an empty birdbath in the garden behind his office.

"Here is what we are going to do," Dr. Cone said. "We are going to send these words back to her." We prayed for my mother, and I told her I loved her and hoped she was happy. Dr. Cone took a match to the letter, and we watched her words and hate float toward the sky in the black smoke.

"Now she has her words back," Dr. Cone said. "They can't hurt you."

I never knew what my mother had written to me, and I never let myself get angry because she had written something that my doctor thought was too painful for me to read. I only felt sorrow for her because she felt so much pain and hurt that her last act was to send me a hate-filled letter from her grave. The man that she invited into our home had beaten her down so much by that she couldn't feel anything other than animosity. Apparently, there was not one drop of motherly love in the letter, and that made me sad for both of us. My mother and I were never able to create the loving bond that many mothers share with their daughters, and the loss of that diminished both of us. Accepting that my mother would never be Mom wasn't easy. Throughout the years, when Mothers' Day cards were at the store, I read a few of the lovely sentiments inside those cards, but I could never relate to those words. The same was true when I would look at a card for my sister. Hallmark only painted the happy side of the page. They never print cards for those of us who don't have the ideal families that we see in magazines and on TV.

After I told Patty about the letter my mother sent me, we sat in the silence, drinking coffee with the smell of the flowers in the small square. Patty turned and said, "Melanie, I want you to know that I would have been proud to call you my daughter."

I was able to fly out of Paris the next morning and return to America. My angel and her husband had another week before they would return to their home in Louisiana. Patty wrote me a few letters after she returned, and we corresponded throughout the years.

God never sends just something. He sends the exact thing you need. God sent Patty into my life when I needed her. She knocked on my door at the specific moment, that specific time to save me.

The Danger I Brought into My House

When Tuxedo Man and I returned to Oklahoma City, things got worse, so bad that the details are still painful and embarrassing to talk about. Almost as soon as we got off the plane, Tuxedo Man said he was driving to Dallas, which is a few hours away, to pick up his daughter at Southern Methodist University. He said that the two of them were going to spend the weekend alone at his lake house.

Family time sounds noble, but the story Tuxedo Man told me was not true. I found out that he picked up his married ex-girlfriend, and the two of them spent the weekend alone.

When he came home Sunday morning, I was sitting on the couch reading the paper. He sat at the other end of the couch and told me that while he was at the lake, he had made a list of pros and cons about me.

"I have made a business decision," he said. "I am divorcing you." To him, our relationship was a series of entries on a ledger, and when he didn't think they added up, it was time to rescind the agreement and enter into a new one.

I am embarrassed to say that I asked him, "Please, don't do it. Let's work on this." I am shocked at how beaten down my spirit and soul were, how tired I had become trying to keep my head held high and my faith intact. I had spent so much energy just trying not to give up that I couldn't imagine a life without him in it.

That is how seductive Evil can be. Tuxedo Man had shown me his true colors, and they weren't pretty. If I had been looking at our relationship through the lens of reason, I would have seen how damaged and damaging the man was. But I was trapped by my own actions, and instead of following the divine path that had been created for me, I had veered off on my own route. I had allowed myself to be distracted by beautiful homes and the thought of an easy, work-free life. I didn't understand that nothing comes without a cost. Evil morphs itself into something desirable and comforting before it tries to take your soul and attempts to devour you.

After I asked Tuxedo Man to stay with me, his reply was, "When I make a business decision, I do not change my mind."

I was devastated. I had quit my job and sold everything I owned to be with him. I had a total of $13.86 in my checking account. To make it worse, I had signed an ironclad prenup that meant I wouldn't get anything in the divorce.

I was comforted by the thought that I had one possession, something that would bring me joy every time I looked at it: the painting we had purchased at the auction. When I drove to the museum to pick it up, I was shocked to hear that they could not give it to me. I was told that because Tuxedo Man had paid for the painting, as far as they were concerned, it was his. Plus, he had threatened the museum with a lawsuit if they gave it to me. I left, hurt and embarrassed, feeling like everything had been taken from me.

A few weeks later, as I was packing and reorganizing the few things I still owned, I came across a pair of gold and ruby cufflinks that had belonged to Tuxedo Man's father. I knew they held a lot of sentimental value, so I went over to his house. Returning those to him was the right thing to do, and I never considered doing anything else with them. When I entered our house, the first thing I saw was his ex-girlfriend. The grill on the patio was smoking, and they were getting ready for dinner. I told Tuxedo Man what happened and gave him the cufflinks. I glanced at the wall and saw "Lady in Red" hanging with a group of other paintings. Assuming that he would be willing to reciprocate my kind gesture, I reached for the painting. As soon as I touched it, he pushed me toward the wall and told me to get out.

We wound up in scuffle, and after I went home, two police officers were knocking on my door. They told me they didn't want to, but they had to take me to the station for questioning. It was clear they didn't think I had done anything wrong, and after a few hours I was back in the comfort of my home. Nothing came from my husband's futile attempt to have me arrested.

The divorce was as difficult as I could have expected. Our attorneys sent Tuxedo Man to two different psychologists, who made him take a test. The two psychologists came back with the same diagnosis. Tuxedo Man had two mental disorders. The first was that he was an extreme narcissist. I had never dealt with a narcissist before, and I didn't know what that meant. I only knew that the man I had married, the person I had tied my future to, was full of anger and was tearing me apart every chance he got.

To understand the kind of person I was dealing with, I did a little research on narcissism and discovered that it is a mental disorder where people think they are more important than they actually are. The Mayo Clinic, one of the most respected hospitals in the world, defines narcissistic personality disorder as "a mental condition in which people have an inflated sense of their own importance, a deep need for excessive attention and admiration, troubled relationships, and a lack of empathy for others. But behind this mask of extreme confidence lies a fragile self-esteem that's vulnerable to the slightest criticism."

The Mayo Clinic also says that the disorder can manifest itself in many ways. "A narcissistic personality disorder causes problems in many areas of life, such as relationships, work, school or financial affairs. People with narcissistic personality disorder may be generally unhappy and disappointed when they're not given the special favors or admiration they believe they deserve. They may find their relationships unfulfilling, and others may not enjoy being around them."

I didn't know it, but I had joined my life with someone who cared only for himself and, unless he was willing to admit he had a problem and seek professional help, would never be able to give me the love he promised.

Most women are not strong enough to deal with narcissists. Narcissists know this, and they choose their victims carefully. Their goal is to dismantle your life so that you have nowhere to go. Fortunately, I was far along in my recovery and had the strength to stand up for myself.

The second issue that came out during our divorce was that Tuxedo Man suffered from the same mental disorder as Jeffrey Dahmer, a serial killer who murdered, dismembered, and sometimes ate his victims. The technical name for this disorder was borderline personality disorder, another condition that effects the way people can relate to others. The Mayo Clinic defines this disorder as "a mental health disorder that impacts the way you think and feel about yourself and others, causing problems functioning in everyday life. It includes self-image issues, difficulty managing emotions and behavior, and a pattern of unstable relationships.

"With borderline personality disorder, you have an intense fear of abandonment or instability, and you may have difficulty tolerating being alone. Yet inappropriate anger, impulsiveness and frequent mood swings may push others away, even though you want to have loving and lasting relationships."

After reading these reports my attorney met with me and told me that I was lucky because if I had stayed with Tuxedo Man much longer, I would have ended up dead in the basement of one of his properties.

During the course of the divorce, I learned how hateful and controlling Tuxedo Man had been and how his mind worked. I thought I knew him, but I didn't understand the whole picture until it was drawn for me. We learned Tuxedo Man had kept a daily journal on me, and my lawyer subpoenaed it. I was shocked to read that my husband had detailed each and every penny I spent. Every time I paid sixty-nine cents for a Diet Coke refill at 7-Eleven, Tuxedo Man entered that into his journal.

That wasn't the end of his obsessive recordkeeping. Every day, he made a judgement as to whether I gave him a good hug or a bad hug and wrote that down. Every time I outran him during our daily runs, which bruised his fragile ego, he made a note. After I saw the journal, I absorbed that information, realizing that he had beaten me so far down in such a short time that I believed I was worthless. He took me to the very bottom.

More dirt came out. My attorney asked my husband if he had ever used prostitutes. Without a moment's hesitation, Tuxedo Man said, "Yes." I had never known this and never would have thought to ask him about it. He admitted that while he was serving in the military, he had hired prostitutes in Vietnam. It turned out that many of the soldiers there had contracted syphilis, and the commander of the base was fed up. "The next soldier who gets a sexually transmitted disease is being shipped home and drummed out of the service," he told his troops. After that, Tuxedo Man found a girl who was willing to service him exclusively. She needed the money to help feed her family, and if she wasn't sleeping with anyone else Tuxedo Man didn't have to worry about any trips to the doctor.

Our divorce was finalized on August 14, 2005. I was left without a cent to my name, but the attorneys, even, Tuxedo Man's, took care of me. As part of the settlement, he had to give me $25,000 to use as a down payment for a house. He wasn't happy about that, and to drive home that point, he didn't deliver the check until the afternoon I was scheduled to close on my new house, September 1st, 2005.

Buying a home solved my housing issue, but I still had to find a way to pay the bills. More angels came to save me. They fed me and put gas in my car. Other people came into my life and asked, "Do you need furniture? I just bought new things and have to move the old ones."

While my life was in turmoil for some time after our divorce, I am eternally grateful that the pros and cons of my life did not allow me to stay tethered to Tuxedo Man.

Despite all the hard work I had done and the progress I made, it was clear that I still had a lot of work to do. I had to accept that life wasn't going to be easy, and that Prince Charming wasn't going to ride in on a white horse and sweep me away to his castle where I would never have to work again. I needed to become the person God wanted me to be by growing my spirit, and I was fortunate to find a therapist who agreed with that course of action. I met with him weekly (at first, two to three times a week) for five years. During some of our early sessions, the most I could do was to sob uncontrollably. I couldn't utter one word. As time passed, I was able to talk about my life and what I had been through. I was able to explain the pain behind my tears.

I grew throughout my recovery, and when the time was right, I moved on to another therapist who was able to help me, and then another. Each therapist that came into my life raised me to the next level and then the next. This process was the pinnacle of my recovery, healing and truly life changing me as a person. At least that's what I thought.

Rebuilding

"Rejection is the Universe's way of protecting you."
Deganit Nuur

Divorcing Tuxedo Man saved my life, but it left me with the prospect of being homeless. Literally. I had nothing but a comforter and a pillow I had saved from the home I owned before marrying Tuxedo Man. I had sold the rest of my belongings at his request. "Why do I need anything of my own?" I thought at the time. I would never have to work again, we would travel the world together, and we could split time between homes he owned in three different states.

Sounds good, doesn't it? Lies always do, especially when you are broken and weak.

My marriage was over, and I was left with almost nothing. I was in shock. How could this happen to me? I am an intelligent woman with a college degree. I had resigned from an upper management position with a Fortune 500 company that paid me a good salary. I went from owning my own home and a nice car to having nothing, nothing at all, in the blink of an eye. It had taken only three months for my life to be leveled in every way possible.

The worst thing was that I had done this to myself. I became weak and took a bite of forbidden fruit. I had disconnected from Heaven, from God, from Christ Jesus, and from the Holy Spirit, all of whom had been watching over me. My brain could not process how far I had fallen.

I couldn't allow myself to be wrapped up in self-pity. I knew that God uses people who walk with Him because so many people reached out to me with love and kindness, people who helped me dig my way out of the numerous holes I dug for myself. But the Devil does the same. He entices people to lead others off the path that God wants them to follow. Tuxedo Man had been sent by the Devil to keep me from receiving all the blessings that God had prepared for me. Even though that marriage was a traumatic experience, I had to embrace the fact that it was another step on my path, and there was no reason for me to deny that it had been part of my life.

Although I did not understand it at the time, by ignoring my pleas to keep my marriage together, God was saving me from imminent danger and most likely death. God had a plan to get me back on my feet. It was a plan that would put me in a better position in every way better than I had ever been in my life.

There is a line from a song by country music singer Garth Brooks: "Some of God's greatest gifts are unanswered prayers." He could have written that line about me. There were so many times that I fell to my knees and asked God for the wrong things, things that I would have given all that I owned to possess. They were destructive things, but when God protected me by denying me what I asked for, I was disappointed that He wouldn't let me have them. The reality is that He was keeping me safe and on the path to be with Him for eternity.

The Angel with a Credit Card

"Everybody has a breaking point."
General Joseph Martin, Chief of Staff

We may all have breaking points, but they are different for each of us. I found out what mine was when I was sitting in a hotel room in Paris wondering if I was going to live to see Oklahoma again. My experience with Tuxedo Man was terrifying and humbling, but it was also a point of closure. The end of that journey wrapped up past stages of my growth and helped me become healthier than I was before.

After Tuxedo Man was out of my life, it didn't take long for me to see miracles happening around me. Within one month of my divorce, God put me in a home that was twice as nice as the one I had sold four months earlier. It is located in one of the most affluent, historic, and safe neighborhoods in the city, and I didn't spend one cent of my own money to move in.

How did that happen? I woke up laying on the floor of this house with nothing but my pillow and comforter asking myself that question. I looked around the bedroom and thought, "I guess I live here now."

I had few memories of how I got from Point A to Point B, of how I came from sobbing my eyes out in a hotel room in Paris to owning a new home in Oklahoma. My brain didn't want me to suffer, so it took those memories, encapsulated them, and filed them away so I will not relive that trauma.

I believe that God built these responses into us because He loves us. He knows from the time He spent on Earth in a physical body that humans have the capability to inflict evil on each other in ways that are beyond comprehension. He knows we will suffer pain throughout our lives and does not want us to recall traumatic experiences so that we will stay safe and happy.

I do remember finding a home I liked, making an offer that was accepted, and using the check that Tuxedo Man was forced to pay as a down payment, but many of the other events that happened during that time of my life have been forgotten.

Buying that home solved the issue of housing, but it didn't mean I could sit around and do nothing. I had to find a way to pay my bills and keep a roof over my head.

I didn't have any money or equipment, so I had to make money with my skills and talents. I have an innate organizing mind. As I child, I enjoyed organizing the books in my bedroom. I can look at a space and visualize ways to make it better. I have no idea where that comes from, but I knew I could use it to make a living. I started a company called OrganizeThisStuff.com. I told my hairdresser about it and gave her my cell phone number to handout to anyone who might be interested.

When I wasn't focused on making money, there were other financial details to deal with. I needed to call USAA, a credit card company, to let them know I was divorced and that I no longer had the credit card Tuxedo Man had given me through his account.

A kind customer service woman answered. I told her what happened and started crying. She told me not to worry. She said that because I had married Tuxedo Man, I had certain benefits with USSA. Those benefits could not be taken away, even if we were divorced. One of those benefits was that I could have a credit card issued in my own name, and the card could be issued without a credit report check or a job verification. She said she could send me the card via overnight delivery, and I would have it the next day. She also mentioned that the card would have a credit limit of $30,000.

What? I couldn't believe that had been dropped into my lap. It was a godsend.

I shouldn't have been surprised. Once again, God was watching over me and sending angels to care for me. Thank you, Jesus. God doesn't bring just something. He brings exactly the thing you need at the time you need it.

That credit card saved my life. I used it to buy food, put gas in my car, and pay the utility bills. My business took off, and I was busy organizing offices and homes.

I looked for other ways to make money. If there was a dollar to be made, I was interested. When my son had been a junior in high school, I knew I would be bored once he left and the nest was empty, and one of my friends recommended that I get my real estate license. She thought I would be good at it, and that once my son moved out it would be a way for me to stay busy and make some money. I never got a chance to use it because not long after I passed the exam, I took a job at Omnicare, a healthcare company, and didn't have the time to sell real estate. After my divorce from Tuxedo Man, I activated that license so that I could sell houses.

My company helped people organize when they moved into a new home. I boxed up their things at their old houses and unpacked their belongings in their new ones. I organized the house and all their furniture. All they had to do was show up at their new home and everything was ready to go.

Word got around, and people who hired me began to tell their friends what a great job I did for them. I began to earn enough money to keep my head above water.

I had gone from living on the floor of a rental home to buying a new home, from being unemployed to having my own business that was growing and keeping my bills paid. I had survived by the grace of God and His love for me.

God didn't stop there. His angels kept showing up, and some of them showed up more than once.

My hair stylist called and said she had given my cell number to Linda, a woman who needed help organizing a few things. Linda called me to organize and set up her home office, which was in a new condo she had purchased. I took the job and showed up the next day.

When Linda opened the front door, I was in shock. I recognized her immediately, but she didn't seem to recall me. The last time I had seen her, she was giving me a check for $5,000 to return to my boss. She had seen the pain that was seeping out between my cracks and pointed me in the direction of help and hope.

She showed me where she needed her office to be and the things in her house that needed to be organized. We agreed on the day I would start, and I left. I got in my car and drove to a nearby parking garage. I called my therapist and told her what had happened. I asked if I should tell this woman that we had met before and that she had been an integral part of how I had gone through treatment at Sierra Tucson.

"Do not tell her now," my therapist said. "The right time will present itself to you."

I completed Linda's project, and she was so pleased with the work I did for her that she started referring other people to me. God and his army of angels weren't sitting on the sidelines. They were busy laying the bricks that I would use to build the next part of my life.

Linda sold a man a large two-story house that was about four blocks from my new house. The man, Jack Morgan Field, was travelling for a few months and needed someone to meet his moving van and organize his house. I jumped at the opportunity.

I met the moving van when it arrived. I arranged Jack's furniture on each level, unpacked his kitchenware, clothes, and everything else he sent. I organized and labeled all of it.

After the job was done, Linda paid me, and I went back to work. Linda called me a few weeks later. She said Jack had called her and asked who had done the work at his house.

"Was there a problem?" Linda asked.

"No," Jack said. "I have just never seen anything like this. My shirts are folded, my socks are in the drawer are arranged by color. My clothes are organized by color and sleeve length. I want to hire this person."

Linda asked if it was okay for her to give Jack my cell phone number. I said yes, and he called me right away. We decided on a day and time for us to meet. Jack told me he operated an oil and gas company that owned minerals and oil and gas leases in twenty-two counties across Oklahoma. I told him that in my twenties, I had worked for the president of an oil and gas company, but it was on the drilling side. I held the job for eight years and knew quite a bit about the industry.

Jack had an office in town but did not like to go there to sign division orders or leases. He wanted to hire me to go to his office, pick up any documents he needed to sign or review, bring them to him, and take the signed documents back to his office.

I accepted the offer. We decided on an hourly rate, and the schedule would be flexible enough so that I could still do my other jobs. He would call when he needed me to pick up something and deliver it to him.

One of my qualities that Jack liked was that if you call me and I do not answer, I call you right back. That is how I was trained when I worked in the corporate world. I always have worked this way. My coworkers and clients depended on this.

As Jack and I worked together, we talked, and he became aware that I was recovering from a drastic change in my life and getting myself back on track financially. I may have owned a nice house in a nice neighborhood, but that was about it. I didn't have much on the inside. If a thief had broken in, he might have felt sorry for me and left me a few dollars for me to get something nice for myself.

"This should never have happened to you," Jack told me. He understood the misery that I had suffered and saw what I had gone through. He didn't like the furniture in his house, and as he replaced the furniture in it, he gave me some of his old items, including a couch and a flat screen TV. He even had his old couch delivered by the furniture store that dropped off his new one. I was no longer sleeping in an empty house, and

I was grateful that Jack had stepped up to be one of my angels. He did these things without any judgement or expectation of being repaid. He was simply one human being helping another human who was in need.

Linda was a phenomenally successful real estate agent at a large firm in town. One day, she said, "I wish you had your real estate license, because I would love for you to work on my team." I told her I did have a real estate license, but I had never done anything with it. I started working under Linda's broker's license at Caldwell Banker.

Linda invited her real estate partner, Kathy, and me to lunch. I was thrilled to go, because it meant I would not have to pay for a meal. Every penny mattered, and that invitation meant I could save a few dollars. At the restaurant, I listened to the two of them talk about the closings they had scheduled. Then Linda said to me, "I don't know you, but I am impressed by your work and would like you to partner with me and Kathy."

A voice in my head, which I now know was the Holy Spirit, whispered to me, "Tell her now." I looked at Linda and said, "You do know me. You met me in 1986 at a lunch meeting and said I was making you crazy."

At first, she didn't know what I was talking about. Then it came to her. She was stunned. They both were. We all just sat there, shocked, not saying anything.

How did something like this happen? How did our paths cross after so many years? How was she led back into my life? The only answer that makes sense to me is that we were placed together by the hand of God.

I accepted Linda's offer and the three of us started working closely together. We helped each other show houses and prepare contracts for sales. I was still running my organizing and moving business and was getting referrals from other real estate agents. I was busy and felt blessed to have so much work. It was a welcome change after being worried about where my next meal was coming from.

A few weeks went by, and I was still reeling from the previous four months of my life. I needed to heal from the abrupt end to my whirlwind marriage. That's the thing about love that blows in unexpectedly. It looks like a cooling breeze, but it quickly becomes a tornado and destroys everything in its path. Eventually, it will be up to you and you alone to pick up the pieces and create a new life.

I thought that because I was away from my ex-husband that I was out of the storm, but the damage he had done was tearing me apart on the inside. I needed to deal with that in order to rebuild. I put on a brave face to tell the outside world that all was well with my soul, but that didn't work. My pain was obvious to everyone around me.

We were in Linda's car one day going to show a house or taking care of some other business. I must have been a wreck, visibly showing the signs of a person having a mental breakdown. Instead of dealing with the harm that had been inflicted upon me, I tried to force it down inside me by exercising as much as I could. I weighed ninety pounds. In the car with Linda, I was shaking and talking 100 miles an hour. It must have been difficult for her to be in a confined space like a car with someone who had so much nervous energy.

Linda looked at me and said, "I cannot help you, but I know some-one who can." She called someone on her cell phone and said, "I have a woman who is in crisis in my car. I'm bringing her to your office."

I had no idea who this person was or where I was going, but I trusted Linda. I must have known, on some deeper level than I was capable of understanding at the time, that Linda had been sent to help me again. Linda drove to an office and told me the staff was expecting me.

I walked in, and the person at the front desk said he would tell him I was there.

Him who?

Moments later, an exceedingly kind and gentle man came out and introduced himself as Dr. Gary Cone. I could feel an incredible energy, a strong spiritual energy, radiating from him. We went into his office. I sat down.

"Did Linda tell you what I do?" Dr. Cone asked.

"No," I said. The truth is I had no idea of why I was there, but I trusted Linda. Within minutes, I felt an inner peace that let me know I was supposed to be in that office at that moment.

Dr. Cone said he was a therapist, but instead of treating patients with traditional methods or medicines, he came from more of a spiri-tual path.

Something whispered to me. This man was part of my path. I was in the right place to take the next part of my journey.

Because I was convinced that I had been led to this healer by God, I jumped in with both feet. I spent the next five years seeing him three times a week, then two times a week, and then once a week. He became my therapist, spiritual teacher, and mentor. Most importantly, he became my friend. To this day, I see him every December, just to check in and talk about anything I might need. These meetings are part of my selfcare. Dr. Cone is the reason that I reconnected with God, and he taught me how to heal from all the damage in my life and how to move past the hurt I had caused myself.

For the first several years of our relationship, I constantly asked Dr. Cone, "Why? Why did so many bad things happen to me? Why did I constantly wind up in terrible relationships?" I wanted and needed to understand the cause of my suffering.

He told me again and again, "Melanie, 'Why?' is a question you cannot ask."

At the time, I wasn't mature or emotionally strong enough to understand this or to let things go. I could not accept that answer, and I continued to ask questions.

His answer was always the same. "'Why?' is a question you cannot ask."

The more he said that the more I needed an answer, some clarity on why I had gone through so many challenges. I needed the one solution that would answer all of my questions, a magic wand that I could wave over my life and achieve inner peace and get to the core of who I am.

But that is not how it works. As they told me at Sierra Tucson in 1986, the work I did in inpatient treatment was only 10 percent of the work I needed to do. The other 90 percent would be done in the real world when I got home. It was going to be messy and dirty, and there were no shortcuts. That's what my therapist was trying to tell me, but I didn't want to hear the answer. Healing takes a lifetime and asking questions like "Why?" are ways we try to find simple solutions and avoid the hard work it takes to heal.

But the work is worth it. If you put in the effort, you can become happy, joyous, and free. Your reward is a peace that passes all understanding.

The View from My Grave

The thing about growth is that it doesn't happen all at once. You have to take a lot of small steps, not one giant leap. When you are raised in an unhealthy home like I was, you have a long way to go. When you make any progress at all, it seems like you have travelled miles and are near your destination. The truth is that none of us ever reaches the end of our path. As long as we are breathing, we need to be growing.

I had grown quite a bit throughout the years, growth that came from a lot of blood, sweat, and tears. But I still had a mountain of pain inside me, pain that would rear its ugly head and destroy me if I left it unattended. I had lowered the volume on many of the voices and thoughts echoing in my mind, but they still had influence.

I have learned that I will be working on myself for the rest of my life. I can never let my guard down, or the enemy and the thoughts that had been planted in my brain when I was a child will rise up and try to defeat me again. I put all my time and energy into growing and didn't let anything distract me from that.

I stayed single for seventeen years. There was no dating. Instead of looking for someone to love me, I learned to love myself and to find value in the person I am. I discovered I don't need a man to make me whole or happy. The power to be those things lay in my hands, and I could and would determine who and what I would become.

For four of those years, until December of 2010, I continued with Dr. Cone. I would have stayed with him forever, but one day he told me I was finished. I had stayed longer than most people dare to. He said I had reached the core of the onion, there were no more layers to pull back to find the real me. We agreed that I would come in every December for a "check-up," but I had grown to the point that meeting with him on a regular basis would not be necessary.

My therapist saw it sooner than I did, but he was right. I had grown. I appreciated how blessed and happy I was, and that I had the right to feel that way.

I took stock of my life and calculated how I had spent my life. My history in numbers from the time I was eighteen until October 5, 2020, looked like this:

Total years I had been married:	Sixteen years, five months, one day
Total years I had been single:	Thirty-one years, six months, 364 days
Years after I went to Sierra Tucson:	Thirty

I should have been able to look at those numbers and rejoice in my growth. But the pain and anger were never far away. On April 5, 2006, I could no longer ignore my pain. I was exhausted and didn't want to go forward. Despite all of my work and the progress I had made, I was too tired to continue. I wanted the struggle to be over and to not have to worry about overcoming challenges.

I was sliding into a darker and darker mental state of mind. In the evenings, I would lay on the couch, and when I was not crying, I was sleeping. I was lethargic and was not feeling right. Something was off, but I was in such a difficult place I could not pull myself out of it. My mind was not able to process and realize what was wrong with me.

I got off the couch and went to the bathroom to take the antidepressants my doctor had prescribed for me. I reached into the cabinet behind the sink and looked at myself in the mirror, staring into my eyes. I took a tube of my lipstick and wrote in big letters on my mirror, "I thought it was real."

Then it felt like someone or something was moving my right arm. The entire bottle of pills emptied into my hand.

I swallowed them.

I came out of whatever fog I had been in. I looked at myself in the mirror again and asked, "What have I done?" But it was too late. I became tired, so tired I couldn't stand up. I rested on the couch my boss Jack had given me out of kindness. That's the last thing I remember.

Then I died.

When I crossed over to the light, my first feeling was that I was home. I was where I was supposed to be. It was familiar. I knew I had been there, that it was where I had come from, that it was my true home. I felt a joy I have never experienced in this physical world.

What do parents want when their child goes wayward and they are out in the world, lost? They want their children to come home. The day I died I learned God wants the same thing. He wants us to come home. That is why He left us in the physical world, so He could go back to where

He came from to get ready for our homecoming. He is preparing a place for us to dwell with Him for eternity.

You might not be able to fathom these ideas. I still have a hard time understanding all the lessons I realized when I was dead.

My weakness on that day had opened a crack in my soul. It was a small crack, no more than a sliver, but evil doesn't need much room to slither into your life. That small opening gave Satan the opportunity to attack me. The next thing I knew, I was writing in lipstick on a mirror and swallowing a handful of pills.

Fortunately, God stepped in again. He used the horrible choice I made and used it to help me grow.

My death reinforced my belief that Jesus died on the cross to save my life. God's amazing grace began to work on me that day. God knew what was happening in my life, and He let me visit Him. I heard His voice. There was a bright light that had all the colors of the rainbow. It drew me in. It was comforting and love emanated from it, a love strong and sweet, a love I never felt before.

I desperately needed that experience. I needed to remember whose I was. I needed to be reminded that I was His. I didn't want to leave so I pleaded to God, "Please let me stay with you. Please let me stay."

I didn't get the response I wanted. "Not yet, Melanie," God said. "I have work for you to do." I realized that God knew my name, and that made me feel like His child. Then He sent me back.

My visit to the other side proved to me that God loves us, and it validated the miracles He gives us. It confirmed beyond a shadow of a doubt that there is a God, a God who understands us and wants us to be happy, a God we can rest our hopes and dreams on. He is a God we can lean on when our world turns dark.

I was lucky to have been found. Jack and another of my business contacts had been trying to call me, and when I didn't answer they became alarmed. I had always responded to calls and messages as soon as I could, and my silence concerned them.

I only know the medical details of what happened while I was on the other side because in 2016, I went to the hospital and pulled my medical report. The EMTs in the ambulance put the paddles on my chest eight times on the way to the hospital. In the emergency room, the doctor continued to shock my heart after I flatlined on the monitor and had no heartbeat.

The doctors weren't the only ones doing everything in their power to keep me alive. Jack and the nurse assisting the doctor were standing by me and started praying and begging for me to come back. They thought I was gone forever.

The ER doctor told the people in the room, "Melanie's gone," and he was right. I had crossed over to the other side and caught a glimpse of where we will spend eternity. I can absolutely, beyond one shadow of any doubt, tell you that after we learn our lessons on Earth, we cross over into Heaven to be with the Divine. Our reward for graduating from Earth School is to meet our Heavenly Father.

After what seemed an eternity to Jack and the nurse praying for me, the monitor beeped again. I left the peace and love of our Father's house and returned to my worldly home.

The nurse who had prayed for me came to see me after she learned I was awake in the ICU. She told me she hadn't stopped praying when she was off the clock. When she went home, she started a continuous prayer vigil for three days, interceding on my behalf so that I might live. She said she could not wait to return to work to find out if I was alive. When she learned I was recovering, she asked to see me so she could tell me what had happened. I never knew why she had prayed for me, but it was clear that she was called to lift up my name when I came into the unit.

I was shocked when she told me that the doctor had pronounced me dead in the hospital. I had not told anyone about how I had crossed over and stood in God's presence. I knew what I heard, saw, and felt, but maybe I had been dreaming. When the nurse told me my heart had stopped beating, it confirmed that my time in Heaven had actually happened.

"The bright light and the conversation with God were real," I thought.

When Jack came to visit, I told him what the nurse had said and asked him if it was true. He confirmed that everything the nurse told me was the truth. I had come back from the dead. He said while I was flat-lining, he was holding my hand and saying, "Please come back Melanie. Please come back."

While I was recovering in the ICU, I was treated by a husband-and-wife team of doctors from India. On the first day, the wife started drawing my blood and running various tests.

The same thing happened on the second day. On the morning of the third day, she said, "I know I have been drawing a lot of blood. I looked at all your medical records, and there is nothing in them to explain why you were so tired. Something is wrong. I want to run one more test."

I agreed, and a few hours after drawing more of my blood, the doctor returned. "I found the problem. It's your thyroid. It has shut down. That happens sometimes when a person experiences extreme trauma," she said. "Your thyroid controls everything about your body. It tells your heart to beat, controls your brain, all of it.

"No wonder you thought you were going crazy, and that's why you were so tired all the time. I am going to set you up with a thyroid specialist."

That physician put me on special thyroid medicine. I began to come out of my funk and feel like me again. To this day I take thyroid medicine daily and will have to for the rest of my life. I would not have been diagnosed if I had not been in the hospital. My attempt to end my life had actually saved it.

I now see the amazing miracles God weaved into my life. I am glad I am alive and that I have experienced the full life that has been given to me. Trying to kill myself is not something I ever dreamt I would do, but I am not ashamed or embarrassed to tell my truth. Maybe God called me to be close to Him because He knew I needed to confirm that He is real, a living, loving God. There is joy that came from my decision to commit suicide. It gave me a lesson that I needed to grow, one that has pushed me forward. It was a divinely correct moment for my life and spiritual growth.

I learned a lot of lessons after that experience, mostly because The Holy Spirit has been after me like a bloodhound. He will not let me give up. The most important lesson I learned is that there is a way to live a peaceful and abundant life.

I also learned that the life that we are living here on earth is about one thing: love. Our purpose is to have a relationship with God and for us to know how much He loves us.

Those of you reading this book felt a nudge inside to pick it up. That inner nudge, the small, still voice that told you it might be an interesting read, was the Holy Spirit. You can also call it your intuition, your God spark, or the light inside you. With the right teaching, you can learn to sense the Holy Spirit or intuition and learn.

Spiritual growth happens in levels. When we are ready, we learn one lesson, and then we are ready for the next one. Each phase gets deeper and deeper into building a relationship with God that becomes a part of us, part of who we are as people. A true connection with God is so powerful that people around you can see it. As you grow closer to God, they recognize something about you has changed. They start to ask, "What are you doing? There is something different about you." It's the light inside of you that they are seeing.

I no longer believe in coincidences, and I wondered if there was any meaning to the date of my death. Had I left Earth on a significant moment? I researched the meaning of April 5, 2006 and found the number four represents the cross of Jesus Christ. The number five represents the grace of God, God's kindness and favor to all of us. The number six represents the weakness, the fallenness, of humankind. I took that to remind me of Jesus' grace for all of mankind, a group that is weak by nature. Because of that weakness, Evil finds us when we are the most vulnerable.

Evil is among all of us, a fact that is confirmed by the things we hear every day when we turn on the television or surf the Internet. Our world is at critical mass, it is under attack. Venice is falling underneath the sea. California is burning to the ground. Over a billion animals burned to death in Australia in a fire that raged across the country. Deadly hurricanes have nearly wiped Haiti off the map. Country after country is dragged into war, an endless cycle of violence and depravity. The list of horror goes on and on.

When we hear this news, our human bodies are crippled with fear and anger, and we question why God would do this to us. When we take time to reflect and remember that we are connected to the Source of Life, to God, we are calmed.

We may be surrounded by Evil, but there is another power that envelopes us. There is a force, an energy, a love so strong for me and each one of you that it reaches down from Heaven and says, "Not today, Satan. Not today." When you reach out to God and humble yourself, an invisible hand reaches out, grabs your hand, and leads you to safety. Angels are sent to you to resurrect you from the fires and the ashes of Evil.

God and His angels never fail you, never ever. I know this for sure. When I was smoldering, blackened as defeats set my life on fire, I was able to raise my head and take a breath of fresh air. I felt myself coming alive. Some people do not have to go to the depths that I did, but it took that for me. God knew that. That is why He allowed me, as they say in *The Wizard of Oz*, to look behind the curtain, behind the veil, to feel His presence, and to hear His voice. My death was another piece of God's plan for my life, another class in my Earth School training.

It became clear to me that many times I had believed my plan was better than the one God had designed for me. My mantra was, "I'm going to make the life I want for myself." I was certain I knew how to create a family and to find the children I longed to adopt.

God loved me enough to let me try my plan, and I got the results I deserved. At the moment I was driving over the proverbial cliff, as in *Thelma & Louise*, God reached down, grabbed the collar of my shirt, and pulled me back.

One of the most moving books in the Bible for me is the Gospel of John. I especially like Chapter 14. Jesus has gathered all the disciples in the upper room. It is the night before His Father's plan is about to be carried out. Jesus knows He will be crucified very soon and that He is going away. His disciples are distraught and cannot understand why Jesus would leave them. Jesus tells them that it is better for them if He goes away. They ask, as I would have, too, "How in the world could that be good for us?" Jesus continues to tell them He is going to prepare a place for them so that they can come and be with Him forever.

While He is working on that place, He says the following to them in John 14: 16 &18: "I will ask the Father, God and He will give you another Helper, to be with you forever." "I will not leave you as orphans; I will come to you." That is what I prayed for, someone to love me unconditionally. A person who would absolutely love me, in spite of who I was or who I might become. It was God, and God alone, who loved me like that. There was no physical human being, someone outside of me, who could give me the love I wanted and needed. The only source of unconditional love is our Father in Heaven.

There were many times when I felt like an orphan. My family had rejected me for being honest and for standing up for the truth. I spent much of my life believing that I would never be part of a loving and giving family. I know today that is not true. I was never an orphan. None of us are. God was watching over me every moment of my life. We are part of His family from the moment we were created.

His love is shown all around us. Hebrews 1:4 tells us that angels are messengers used by God, an order of created spiritual beings whose attributes are strength and wisdom. Their ministry is largely devoted to the physical safety and well-being of each one of us.

God assigned special angels to keep me safe, guide me, and watch over me, as He has for you. We each have a guardian angel who is especially assigned to us. I call this our lead angel. Mine is my Grandmother Wyatt. I feel her around me all the time, even though she passed on decades ago.

This is an extreme oversimplification, but our guardian angels have what I call a special email link to God. When they know we need extra help, they type in our name in the subject line. God gets the email, sees our name, and sends the angel directions on how to best assist us in overcoming whatever challenges we are facing.

Sometimes, these challenges come from within. In the past, I have felt disappointment in myself. I was disappointed that I got weak, not only in my physical body but in my spirit as well. God was there but I was not. Like a computer that loses its Internet connection, I had lost mine and my hard drive was down. My anti-virus protection had crashed. I needed to have my RAM wiped clean so that I could reboot and start processing things again.

Old Paint

Have you ever seen an antique cabinet at a garage sale that had different layers of paint and scratches? Could you visualize the way it looked when it was brand new with no paint, no scratches, when it was just beautiful clean wood? Maybe you bought it and started working on it, sanding off one layer at a time. It took a lot of hard work and elbow grease, and at times you didn't think your arms could do any more sanding.

That is what life is like for me. I was born into this world brand new, never hurt, never physically or mentally abused. Never heartbroken by parents, sister, husbands, or child. But I didn't stay that way.

As my life went along, I got layers and layers of paint put on me. I got scratches, dents, and dings. A person put another layer of paint on me and then another, until I couldn't remember how I looked or felt like when I was brand new. I couldn't remember "me" anymore.

By God's grace and love and His plan for my life, one person at a time came into my life and showed me the way I was supposed to live and who I was supposed to be. I fell down a few times throughout my journey. I would strip a couple layers of paint off of me, and then I would slip and allow another layer of paint to be put back on. Then I would get back up and start again.

Even though I was falling, I was learning and sensing when an unsafe person came into my life, someone that I should not be around. I learned to feel this energy the first time I met someone. The hair on the back of my neck would stand up. I felt that and acted on it. I was growing.

Today, all of my scratches, dents, and dings have been repaired. All of my many layers of paint and varnish have been sanded down. I am a brand new, just-created cabinet. My beautiful new wood is back. I am me. The true me, the authentic me without anyone else's paint that they have thrown on me. God's light shines from inside of me and on the people He puts in my path. I am beyond grateful. I am humbled and blessed beyond anything I ever imagined.

That doesn't mean my life is perfect. I get knocked off of the mountain, and I climb back to the top.

One of the biggest lessons I learned is that I had an incredibly low perception of what I was worth. That's what I was taught by the people closest to me when I was growing up. When your parents and your sibling tell you and show you by their actions that you are not valued, it destroys your self-esteem.

When I turned eighteen, my mother and stepfather said, "You are on our own now. We will not help you financially go to college. We won't help you in any way. Goodbye." My mother repeatedly told me I was the reason her marriage to my stepfather was not working. The two of them wanted me out of the house, and they didn't care what they had to do to get me to leave. They believed, or at least convinced themselves, that I was the problem in their relationship, and when I left, I would take their marital problems with me. The sad part is that they never took time to look inside themselves. That would have been too much work. Instead, they took the easy way out and used me as a scapegoat.

When you are eighteen and out in the world by yourself, you do not understand what is driving your decisions and actions. It takes years to unravel that ball of yarn. When you introduce faith-based words to your problems, to your disease, to your flesh-based issues, healing happens.

The road to healing is not easy. It never has been, and it never will be, and that's one of the reasons most people won't follow it through to the end. Many people would rather sit in their own misery than to endure the pain that true growth requires.

Complacency comes with a cost. If you want easy, you will never reach the level of spiritual growth that you are worth, that is your birthright, and that God has planned for you. He is ready to give it to you. He wants you to have that which is your highest and best good. Isn't it odd that most of our lives we accept so much less than we have been given?

The Lady Revisited

I may have lost "Lady in Red" to a narcissistic ex-husband, but I had never forgotten about her. By 2008, things started turning around for me, and I thought I might be able to save a little bit of money to buy a small painting one day. I didn't think I would ever be in a position to own a beautiful piece of art like "Lady in Red" again, but that didn't mean I couldn't buy something to hang on my walls.

Out of curiosity, I searched for Patricia Dobson online and found a gallery that was selling some of her artwork. I noticed that her work had doubled in value, and this reaffirmed my belief that her artwork would forever be beyond my budget. One painting didn't have a price listed, a picture of a bowl next to some pears. I sent an email with my name and contact information.

Within minutes, I received an email from Patricia. "Hello. I know you," she wrote. "You have 'Lady in Red.' That was a birthday present from your husband."

I was shocked. Not only had she responded quickly, but she remembered the night Tuxedo Man "gave" me the painting.

At first, I didn't want to tell her what had happened to the painting, but I thought she had the right to know. After all, it had been her creation, she was the one who had brought it into existence. It had been a part of her life much longer than it had been a part of mine.

We exchanged a few emails over during the following weeks, and I explained where the painting was, and I could feel how angry Patricia was about the way I had been treated. She was appalled by the fact that the painting she had spent months creating was in the hands of someone so cruel and hurtful.

Without me asking, she told me she would paint me another "Lady in Red." I told her I didn't know she could create two separate works of art with the same name or duplicate a painting she had already sold, but she told me not to worry. She would paint another painting that was similar but not identical to the first one. It would be different enough so that no one could complain. Plus, the new painting would be titled "The Lady in Red." She assured me that adding one word to the title would protect us.

Patricia then told me that she had been praying for me and my situation, and that during her prayers she had been told to help make the situation right. Creating another painting for me was her way of obeying that call. She also told me that she would charge me the same price Tuxedo Man had paid for the original painting, despite the fact that her work had become much more valuable over the years. I gave her a down payment and was thrilled to get started.

She wanted to start by locating the sixteenth-century pot that had been used in the first painting. She had borrowed it from a dealer she knew well, but she wasn't sure if it was still available five years after the first painting had been sold.

A few days later, I received an email from Patricia. She told me that the pot had been sold, but the buyer had a change of heart and recently brought it in for the man to sell. It was a gift from above, a sign my angels were looking out for me.

Patricia said she would use the pot for inspiration and would keep me posted as the project moved along. She told me it would take eight to ten months, and I waited for her to work her magic.

In November, I received an email from Patricia telling me the painting was done. She had worked night and day to finish the painting because she wanted me to have it by Christmas.

She also asked if I wanted to come to Scottsdale to see the painting as it was crated and shipped. Of course, I wanted to. That was a no-brainer.

Then she asked, "Do you have any interest in buying the pot that I used in the painting?"

I thought that was a great idea, but I couldn't afford the $4,200 they asked for it. A few days later, Patricia let me know that she had talked to the shop owner, and he agreed to reduce the price to $2,700. I got her a cashier's check for the pot and the balance I owed for the painting, booked my plane ticket to Scottsdale and a hotel room at the Venetian, and headed out for one of the most amazing healings I had experienced in my life.

Patricia met me in the lobby of the hotel, and we wrapped our arms around each other and cried.

A few months later, Patricia called to ask if I wanted to buy the sister pot to the one that was used in the painting. She had seen it while she was looking for small Indian shoes for another painting and thought I might be interested.

Both pots are in my house today. The pot that was used in the painting sits next to "A Lady in Red" under glass on a special shelf I had installed. To people who don't know my story, they are two interesting pieces of art that are prominently displayed in the corner of my living room. To me, and to my friends who know the road I have travelled, they are reminders of the angels who have graced my life and helped me heal.

Fear

*"For God has not given us a spirit of fear, but
of power, of love and of a sound mind."*

2 Timothy 1:7

Fear is one of Satan's most powerful tools, but many of the things we fear are illusions. There is an acronym for fear that defines how it operates in reality: False Evidence Appearing Real. When fear takes over, we no longer see things as they are. Fear forces our minds to react in ways designed to protect us. When you are afraid, your mind no longer thinks with logic or ponders long-term consequences. Its only concern is to get you safely out of whatever situation is causing the fear.

When I have been in that "fight or flight" response, I could not make decisions out of reason. Like you, I wasn't designed to operate that way. I know that now. I have also learned that fear and my response to it can be used against me. When I have a strong sense of fear telling me not to try something, like writing this book, that is Satan trying to stop me. When I think those thoughts, I take a breath and forge ahead with the strength that God gives me. I remember that God is by my side. That pushes fear out of my way and allows me to go forward.

God said He would never leave us, but He lets us choose the paths we take. I have chosen a different path than the one God wanted me to take many, many times. On those occasions, when I adopted Melanie's plan instead of God's, I was trying to force things to happen. This included trying to create that family I wanted, a perfect one that could replace the damaged one I had been born into. My approach never worked, and it was especially dangerous when I allowed my physical body to enter the picture. I was not waiting for my life to unfold in a natural way, and my results show that.

God gives us free will, and the flipside of that is that we get the consequences of our actions. If we choose wisely, we experience peace and joy. If not, we are left with pain and regret. Learning to accept consequences is one of the many ways God teaches us. Developing wisdom to make better choices is how we grow spiritually, mentally, and emotionally.

Our relationships, whether they are with family, spouses, or friends, are part of our Earth School. They teach us many of the lessons we have to learn in order to live with the peace and joy God has given us. It is up to us to open the box and enjoy those gifts. God often uses relationships to take us from kindergarten to college in Earth School. He knows relationships are an integral part of our human existence, and they are the perfect teaching tool. How does God know? He became flesh and dwelt among us. He knows the power of loving friendships and how they can transform our lives. He wants a relationship where we love Him as much as He loves us.

No human knows more about love than our Father in Heaven does. Can you imagine the depth of love that allows a man to be beaten, dragged through the streets with thorns pressed into His skull, and put up on a cross so men could hammer nails through His hands and feet? All of that was a way of showing unconditional love for you and for me, a promise that we could all be with Him in eternity. Could you do that for Him? Could you do that for anyone you say you love? Could I withstand the pain He endured? No matter how long I stay in Earth School, I will never have the knowledge or wisdom to answer those questions.

I had the privilege of visiting Israel with a church group a few years ago. We visited many of the places that were significant to Jesus. After being in Jerusalem and seeing where Christ gave up His last breath for all of humanity on a rough wooden cross, I know I would have been terrified if I had been the one hanging on it. When I knelt and touched the rock where His cross was placed the day He died, I began sobbing. How could they have done this to Him? How could this have happened?

Then I remembered it was all part of His Father's plan. It was the only way to save me and you, all of us. That is the definition of the greatest love there can be. It has always been about us. God wants us to come back home to where we started, to be with Him. But we have to make the choice to be with Him, and when we don't, our lives can fall apart. Much of my life has been a testament to that idea.

Boots for the Trucking Man

I may have been able to find a surrogate mother in Patty, my angel in Paris, but I never had the chance to create a real bond with my mother. That dream ended when she and my sister ambushed me with a lawyer and tried to force me to sign documents formally ending our relationship.

I didn't have such a difficult time when it came to repair my relationship with my father. He may have left my mother and married another woman, but as the years passed, he and I became closer.

As Dad aged and knew he was having difficulty taking care of himself, he decided to make my sister his power of attorney. He told me the reason he had done it was because she was the oldest child, but the truth is he would have chosen her regardless of who was older. He had the right to choose whoever he wanted, and I had no right to complain as long as he was being cared for.

He had built a good life for himself. While he was driving trucks, he bought forty acres outside of Oklahoma City, and when he retired, he sold those to a developer who built a retirement community. Dad was living in one of those condos and was doing well. He had made friends with some of the other residents, and many of them had a coffee clutch where they discussed whatever was going on in their lives and in the world. He had access to great nurses and medical care. There were only three men in the community, and all of the women loved cooking for Dad. It was a great situation for him, and I envisioned him spending the rest of his life there.

When he was ninety-three, I called Dad on a Saturday, but he didn't pick up his cell phone. That wasn't unusual, and I didn't think anything about it. When I called his house phone and got a message that the line had been disconnected, I jumped into my SUV and raced to his house.

I wasn't prepared for what I learned.

I was told that my sister and her husband had flown out from California, and she had put her name on all of Dad's accounts. A neighbor told me that Dad had been taken in a white van to a different center.

I was able to track him down, and he finally answered his phone. "I don't know where I am," he said.

When I went to visit, I was shocked at how different this facility was from the home he had been living in. The door was locked, and while I was waiting for it to be opened, I heard barking and screaming. It turned out that one side of the facility was a mental ward, and Dad was living with people who suffered from a variety of psychiatric illnesses. Instead of having a private home like he had been used to, Dad was sharing a room with a man who was 103 years old.

The first time I saw Dad he was in a wheelchair, with tears flowing down his face.

"I made a terrible mistake," he said to me. "Look at what your sister has done."

Dad called his attorney, and he set up an appointment for me at 10:00 a.m. the next day. We revised his power of attorney, and I was happy to be put in charge of his affairs. We had to have two witnesses who had no financial interests in Dad's estate. One of Dad's friends had a daughter and son-in-law who agreed to be witnesses, and a notary from the bank was happy to come to the nursing home during her lunch break so that we could sign the documents in front of her.

Even though I was Dad's POA, it wasn't easy to get him out of the facility my sister had forced him into. When we tried to leave, one of the nurses refused to unlock the door. "You can't go," she said. After ten minutes of back and forth, a nurse finally let us out.

It was just in time. Dad was so stressed from the change and the chaos in the nursing home that he hadn't eaten for five days, and he had sores from falling. He wouldn't have survived there much longer.

I had to pack up all of Dad's things, and that's when I realized how few belongings my sister had brought for him. He only had some sweatpants, a few T-shirts, and his medication. All his other belongings had been left behind.

We went back to his old house and discovered that virtually everything else Dad had owned had been given away. My sister had hired one of the neighbors to clean the house, and she told the neighbor that she could have everything in it. This included Dad's collection of expensive and exotic cowboy boots and his Lincoln. There was no furniture in the house. It had been picked clean.

I got to work to get Dad back in the situation he deserved. I hired around the clock nurses, and they agreed to start the next day. I had a hospital bed delivered and went to Walmart to get the basic things Dad would need to be on his own. I got him a new cell phone because my sister had cancelled his service.

I also had to buy a safe for Dad's medications. As we were getting things ready, I noticed some of his pills seemed to be missing. There weren't as many painkillers as I expected there to be. I asked Dad about this.

"I had to hide them. Betty has been stealing them," he told me. Betty was a neighbor we had trusted to take care of Dad. He said he had hidden some pills in his cowboy boots, but those were long gone with all his other belongings.

We put the safe in the house and locked the medications in it, and it wasn't long before Betty showed up carrying her little dog. She saw the safe and looked at us.

"What the hell is this?" she asked. The RN and I told her it was to keep the medicine safe, and Betty walked out the door with her dog and never came back.

We had to find where the meds that had been put in Dad's boots had gone, because they included powerful painkillers. We didn't want those to wind up in the wrong hands, and I started tracking down who could have taken the boots. I finally found the person, and she told me the boots had been donated to a home for troubled boys. It was one of the worst places those boots and the stash inside of them could have landed. There was no telling what a house full of young men with behavioral problems would have done with those drugs.

I was upset by those things, but my sister had done something that angered me even more. She had paid for Dad to be cremated. My mother had been cremated, and some of her ashes sit on my sister's mantle in Northern California alongside those of my nephew.

The idea of cremation didn't upset me. The problem I had was that Dad never wanted to be cremated when he graduated from Earth School. My sister had ignored what he wanted to do and replaced his vision with her own.

Dad shouldn't have been living by himself. After my mother and Dad ended their relationship, Dad married Joan, a waitress he met when he was driving trucks in and out of Chicago.

Although I didn't like it when Dad and Joan got together, I came to love her dearly. She was always kind to me, and she held my head and gave me crackers and warm 7-Up when I was sick.

She also taught me one of the best life lessons I ever learned. "If you can look yourself in the mirror when you brush your teeth and feel good about yourself, you've done the right thing," she said.

When I was older, Dad and Joan hosted an annual Christmas dinner, and it wasn't what you would expect. We had to make several stops visiting different houses and sharing the joy of the holidays with friends and family. Dad and Joan's house was always the last, and they knew we couldn't stomach another bite of turkey or stuffing. Every year, they prepared an Italian feast for us. It was relaxing, a special time to spend with each other during the holidays.

Although they seemed to have a good relationship, somewhere along the way things went sideways and Dad and Joan divorced. A few weeks later they realized they had made a mistake and set a date to remarry in Hawaii. Unfortunately, the COVID pandemic put those plans on hold, and they hadn't been able to remarry before my sister dragged Dad out of his home.

While Dad and Joan were married, they had been wise enough to plan their funerals and had bought a plot together. They paid for a custom headstone, which had their names and places for dates that would be filled in when they passed away. The headstone also had a carving of them sitting in a truck, with the words, "Taking a trip" above them. It was a beautiful way to remember Dad and his second wife.

I called the funeral home that was supposed to do the cremation and explained that Dad had never wanted to be cremated and that he never would be. There was no way the cremation was going to move forward.

"But your sister has already paid us," the lady explained to me.

"I don't care," I said. "You can refund her money or keep it. It's your decision. But he will never be cremated."

Not long after, my sister called Dad. I hadn't told her that Dad had been moved out of the place she had put him, but someone else probably had.

"Aren't you happy?" my sister asked.

"You have no idea what you have done," Dad told her.

It was late in the year, and Thanksgiving wasn't far away. "Could you cook Thanksgiving dinner?" Dad asked me.

I told him I would be happy to, and he told me exactly what he wanted: turkey, brown gravy, hot rolls, pecan pie, and the special candied yams that Joan used to make. I said I would need to call her to get the recipe for those.

"Ask her if I could still be buried in our plot," he said.

I called Joan and told her what had happened. Before I could even finish the question, she agreed to let Dad be buried next to her.

"Good. Now I need your yam recipe," I said.

Dad, one of his nurses, and I had a great Thanksgiving meal, and it came just at the right time. The next day, his legs started swelling and the caregivers had to put a catheter in him.

I received a call while I was at home. "I think you need to come," Dad's RN told me.

When I arrived, I held his hand and was stunned at how cold he was. It wasn't long before his urine was tainted by blood.

I sat with him, uncertain of how much more time we would have together. For the most part, he was quiet. The caregivers said he had been nonverbal for some time.

They sent me to Walmart to get some things, and when I came back, one of the nurses told me that Dad had been talking about working on trucks.

Later, his RN told me that hearing is the last of our senses to go. As someone is about to cross over to the other side, they can hear things even after they quit talking. About the same time, Joan called, and I told her what was happening. She wanted to have a few last words with the man she loved, and I put her on speakerphone and held the phone to Dad's ear.

"Bill, you go ahead. It's gonna be fine," she said. "I'll meet you there shortly. I love you."

After nearly eight hours of stillness, Dad said in a voice that was as clear as it had ever been, "I love you too, baby."

In the middle of the night, I got a call from the caregivers who told me that Dad was gone. He had graduated from Earth School and had passed on to the next level. The funeral home was called, and his mortal shell was taken away.

I had a lot of feelings to process after Dad passed away. I could have been angry at my sister. She had abused Dad when he was at his most vulnerable and didn't seem to care what impact that would have on his spirit or his body. But her actions were also a blessing because they gave me the chance to spend time with my dad and give him the unconditional love he deserved. His eyes were opened, and he was able to see I wasn't the problem child that my sister and mother had painted me to be. I had spent two weeks with him night and day, and he was able to see through all the lies.

During his last days, Dad told me that my sister said I was the crazy one in the family, that everyone would be better off if I weren't in the picture. But Dad wasn't buying it after he saw how differently the two of us had treated him. "I have two daughters," he told the nurses. "One of them is bad. The other one I wouldn't trade for a basket full of puppies."

My sister and her husband were not invited to the funeral, which was what Dad wanted. I attended with some of my friends, as did Joan and her two daughters. Joan's pastor came and delivered a beautiful service.

Dad and Joan had considered "Walk Through This World with Me" by George Jones as their song, and it was played at the service. Dad was buried in a blue coffin with an eighteen-wheeler carved into it.

He and Joan had a special relationship, and they often did things that surprised the people around them. While on a vacation at a casino, Dad noticed a gift he wanted to give Joan, and he bought it. Joan also found a gift she wanted for Dad and bought it. It turns out they bought matching watches. The gifts were intended to be surprises, and they had never mentioned them to each other, but they were so connected that they managed to pick the same gift for each other.

The watch Joan had given Dad meant so much to him that he wanted it to be with Joan's watch after he passed away, and she has them together under glass in her living room.

A few days after Dad's funeral, my thoughts turned to my sister. We might never be best friends, but there was no reason I couldn't be civil to her. "We are sisters, after all," I thought. I texted her a photo of the graveside service, Dad's coffin, and all the flowers with a note saying that Dad died surrounded by love and kindness.

Four days later, I received a large envelope in the mail from my sister. It was full of family pictures, many of them featuring Dad and Joan. I called Joan to let her know what I had and to see if she wanted to look at them.

Joan told me that after my sister's house in Northern California had been burned by a wildfire, she visited Joan and gave her those pictures. "It was like your sister didn't want to be a Harding anymore," Joan said. It seemed like my sister wanted to erase any and all connections between us.

Joan also said that my ex-husband Brad had been coming by to see her. "I missed the good times in our lives," he told her. He was right. Those were great years, and I regret that they ended too soon.

The Greatest Loss and the Greatest Gift

I t didn't surprise me that Jack had been willing to visit me in the hospital and pray for my recovery after I tried to end my life. Over the years that we had worked together, we had become close. He was like family to me, and I believe he felt the same about me. We were like brother and sister. There were never any romantic or sexual feelings between us. Our love was more like the love that a close family shares. We comforted each other. I would have done anything for him, and he would have done the same for me. He didn't have any children to talk with, and that may have been part of the reason we became so close.

What I didn't know was that Jack was having his own struggles. His health had suffered for years. He was once an avid runner and had competed in races around the world. But years before we met, he became ill, and doctors had to remove one of his lungs. He also had a sweet tooth and couldn't resist eating candy. He ate so much of it he became diabetic.

On December 7, 2015, as I was running my normal route, I saw emergency vehicles on the side of the street. I didn't think much of it, until I learned that the police and fire department were there because someone had died in one of our neighborhood parks. Some walkers out for their morning exercise had seen a body beneath trees and called 911.

It wasn't long before I heard that the person had taken his own life, and that person was Jack. I then learned that his suicide had not been a random act. He had put a lot of time and effort into deciding how and when to end his life. When the police entered his apartment to investigate, they found a detailed list he had left for me. It included all the people I needed to call and the accounts I needed to close, such as his cell phone and cable.

He also left me a letter. He asked for my forgiveness and said that the years we worked together were the best ones of his life. He said he was sicker than I knew, and that he was now in a better place.

When we put the pieces together, we realized that he died on the anniversary of the attack on the USS *Oklahoma* in Pearl Harbor in 1941. Jack had timed his death to the exact minute the attack occurred. It was a highly detailed plan that he executed with precision.

It seemed like he was trying to tell Oklahoma how much he disliked it, even though he had lived and operated a successful business here for some time. Part of his problem with the state, or at least with some of the people he knew, developed after his father passed away. Jack watched how poorly his mother was treated after she became a widow. Many of the local women had not accepted her, in part because her natural beauty outshined theirs. Jack never forgot how this made her feel, and he carried this anger throughout his life.

His death devastated me. The thought of losing such a close friend, someone that I saw and worked with closely every day for years, was more painful than I expected.

It was even more painful because he had taken his own life to end whatever pain he was suffering, a pain that I had not seen. I was with

Jack almost every day. Was there something I had missed? If I had paid more attention to him, would I have noticed that he needed help? Could I have saved his life?

These thoughts hounded me for weeks. I was placing blame on myself, taking responsibility for things that were out of my control.

The details of his death never made it into the paper, and it was never mentioned on TV. But the neighborhood Jack and I shared is small and close, and word travels fast. It wasn't long before people were asking me, "Did you hear about the man they found in the park? He killed himself." It wasn't easy to tell them it was Jack. I never asked them how they knew, but it was clear that gossip had started early and travelled fast.

Not long after Jack passed away, while I was still struggling with his death and how it happened, I received some news from his attorney.

"Melanie," Jack's attorney said, "Jack left 100 percent of the company to you. You own it outright." Without my knowledge, over the years Jack had been updating his trust to give me more and more of his company. The attorney told me on Jack's final visit to his office, he had changed his trust to give me all of the company upon his death. That was a nice gesture, one that I never would have expected. I was shocked, especially because Jack had never said one word to me about it.

I was stunned. It was a life-changing gesture. I knew what the company was worth and was surprised that I was suddenly the owner of a multi-million-dollar oil and gas company. I thought about the days when I didn't know how I was going to survive after I had been left with a few dollars in my checking account. I remembered the numerous jobs I worked to pay the bills as a single mom.

There was no time or reason to celebrate. No time because I had to conduct a funeral in accordance with Jack's wishes. It was to be closed to the public, including his brother and sister. When that was complete, I had to go through the normal court proceedings, and part of that meant people could show up and file claims against the estate. At the time he died, Jack owed money to several credit card companies, and I anticipated them showing up in court. To my surprise, none of them did. The thought crossed my mind that his siblings might object to me taking over the company, but they didn't say a word. His brother and sister were both successful in their own right, and they didn't need any of Jack's money. Plus, they knew Jack and I had become genuine friends, and they were happy to respect his wishes.

There was no reason to celebrate, because in order for me to receive this gift, my friend had to die. I hope you understand that if given the choice, I would gladly trade every penny I received from Jack for the chance to be with him again. No amount of money can replace the love of a true friend, and not a day goes by that I don't think about him and how much I miss him.

But I don't have the power to bring him back, even though I would if I could. All I can do is to be grateful for the gift he gave me and use it as an opportunity to share my message with the world.

Thank you, Jack, for blessing me with your friendship and your gifts. I hope and pray I will be a good steward of the treasures that have come my way.

Lessons From My Earth School

After all the ups and downs of my life, I have developed a faith that allows me to connect the dots on all the events that have happened. I look back and see that God has led me to where I am today. There were no accidents, just lessons to help guide me to the life He created for me. Here are some of the most important lessons I was given.

Love

*"Now faith is confidence in what we hope for and
assurance about what we do not see."*

Hebrews 11:1 (NIV)

All of us are born with gifts, things that we can do to help transform Earth into God's kingdom. These gifts include faith and the ability to be a prophet, a pastor, or a teacher. God gave us gifts to equip believers to serve others.

But these gifts will not work by themselves. Love is the glue, the bond that unites the fruit and the gifts that God gives each of us. When you practice your gifts with the fruit of the spirt you will minister to people when they need it the most.

Gifts without love are useless. If you do not have love, people will not hear you, and you will gather adultery, fornication, uncleanness, lewdness, idolatry, jealousies, outbursts of wrath, selfish ambitions, dissensions, heresies, envy, murders, drunkenness, and revelries.

It comes down to who we are listening to. If we listen to God, we can have lives full of peace and love. If we listen to our bodies, to emotion instead of reason, we will destroy ourselves and those around us.

But the most important aspect of the human spirit is this:

The Spirit of Christ indwells the regenerated human spirit.

To put it another way, if the door between our body and our soul is open but the door between our soul and our spirit is closed, we won't have help from the Holy Spirit. We won't have Christ Jesus' input to help us make good decisions. If we are in that condition, we are set up for failure, and life gets messy.

But when we give up our plan and accept the help from our Helper, our fleshly desires are not in control of our lives. When we open the door between our soul and spirit, we are on the path God made for us.

It comes back to having a relationship with God, the friendship that He wants with us. It is like having the answers to a test. You know the proper decision to make on any given thing in your daily life so that you are happy, joyous, and free. When you make the right decisions, you reap the fruits of the Spirit: love, joy, peace, patience, kindness, goodness, faithfulness, gentleness, and self-control.

The message God has asked me to impress upon you that love is all He wants from us. Love is the one and only answer to everything in your time on the Earth. It is all you need to graduate from Earth School with honors.

It is easy to spot people who lack love for one another. They judge one another. Judgment is a person acting out of their fleshly body and not opening the door between their soul and the Holy Spirit. God's input, their Reason, cannot reach them.

I cannot tell you how many times people have judged me. The reason I know is because they have given me their opinions and judged me on my entire life. Granted, I've made plenty of mistakes, and that makes me an easy target for people who would rather lash out at me than work on healing themselves. There is a wonderful phrase I heard and is one that I wished I would have remembered to say at those times: "Don't judge my story by the chapter you walked in on."

No one but me has walked my path, and no one but you has walked yours. We do not know the path that others have been walking. We each have a plan, a path to walk that God has designed for us specifically.

Empathy, kindness, and compassion are what we desire from each other. Those are the actions that will help us travel our roads in peace, love, and joy.

We all experience painful times, heart wrenching times, times when we think we cannot live one more second. When your flesh wants to jump out and make a judgement about a fellow human being, stop and remember that the people around you have had painful experiences and sadness, just like you have. Let us look at each other and say, "You got this. We can finish Earth School together."

The Truth

"The quieter you get, the more you can hear God's voice."

I like that quote. It reminds me that God is present and talking to us. But it also implies that we have to open our hearts and minds so that we can listen to Him. We have an active role to play if we want to be closer to God and hear His truth.

For the longest time, I believed that everyone, truly everyone, wants and desires the truth. As Perry Mason would say, "The whole truth and nothing but the truth." I think of my Grandpa Wyatt when I say that phrase. He was "that guy." When he shook your hand, you could count on his word.

People knew he was going to live up to his end of the bargain. When I was a child, I went with him to the bank when he was purchasing a large John Deere tractor to plow the wheat fields at the farm. We walked in and met with the bank president. The president said, "Hi, Forrest. How can we help you?" My grandfather told him what piece of equipment he needed to purchase. The bank president said, "Sounds good," and they shook hands. I never saw my grandfather sign a single piece of paper. A handshake from my grandfather was his signet ring, a promise that you could take to the bank. Watching him and how he did business formed me into the woman I am today.

I have tried to live a life that was based on and consistent with the truth, and that is one of the reasons that I have tried to be close to God. For decades, I believed the old saying that the truth would set me free. I believed that if I were honest, I could liberate myself.

For the most part, that has been accurate. When I have been honest with myself and lived a life consistent with the truth, I have been at peace and have become more of the person I was designed to be. When I avoided the truth, my life went the opposite way.

I also believed that if I shared the truth with people, they would be set free as well. I believed that being honest with people was a gift, that I was opening my heart in the hopes that we could both have more fulfilling lives.

I was shocked to learn that many people do not want to hear or know the truth. To some, the truth is a threat because it means they have to take responsibility for their actions or face demons they had been battling for years. To others, the truth challenges assumptions they have built their lives around, and they cannot handle the possibility that those ideas could be wrong.

I could not wrap my head around the concept that people did not want to know the truth. I was even more surprised to learn how far some people would go to avoid or reject the truth. When you are honest and share the truth with some people, they will punish you, often severely. I learned this lesson when I was a twelve-year-old girl who needed her mother and to acknowledge the truth about what her stepfather was doing to her. Instead of being embraced with love and support by my family when I brought the truth to the center of our lives, I was shunned. My relationship with my family was never the same after that. The light of the truth peeked out between the cracks of the life my mother was trying to create for herself, even though it was crumbling around her, and she was not able to stop it from illuminating her and the choices she had made.

If you want to become the person God wants you to be, you have to be willing to live by the truth. Jesus promised He would reveal *all* truth to the apostles. But all truth does not mean knowledge. Truth often leads to something else.

A meaningful lesson I was taught is "power by knowledge." True power, unshakable power that is based on truth, is what many people fear. When you show up in a room resonating the truth and shining with light, some people become defensive and will do anything, truly anything, to get you out of the room and away from them. This includes your own family. In fact, your family may be the people who are the most likely to do this.

"You shall know the truth and the truth shall set you free." Being truthful set me free, but it did not set my family free. When I told the truth about what was being inflicted on me, it created anger, denial, and retaliation that spanned decades.

God gave us free will. Sometimes I question whether that was a good idea. But giving us freedom is the way He knows that we love Him. He gave us the choice to love Him or not. As I became healthier, I grew to give people the freedom to choose. I could not make them believe the truth. Some of them were not ready. It was not the time for them to accept the truth. They were not prepared to walk the path I was on, and we had to go our separate ways.

That was not easy to do. When you love a person, such as a family member, you want them to come with you on your journey. I wanted my family to be happy, joyous, and free. I learned I am not that powerful. They each have their own individual divine plan that God has created for them, just as He has for me. I had to let go and let God lead them. He had another job He needed me to do for Him. Letting go was liberating. If you want real control, drop the illusion of control and let life live you. It does anyway.

We are all in Earth School. We have lessons to learn and ways we need to improve ourselves. When we graduate, we move on to be with God in peace, love, and relaxation.

When we leave this planet, all we take with us is soul consciousness. We are all just energy. Our flesh does not cross over with us. We do not need it anymore. It was the house for our energy, a place for our spirit to live in on this earthly plane. Energy does not die. We may lose form, our physical bodies, but we move forward as Spirit and go back to God, back to home. When it leaves our physical bodies, the soul is free. The spirit world does not have duality. It returns to a place of no judgement, a place of healing and comfort.

I vividly remember when I crossed over feeling as light as a feather. I was in the presence of the Ultimate Truth, and I felt free. I was not weighed down by the physical body I had been living in. It was like I was hiking in the mountains carrying a heavy backpack. When I took off that backpack at the end of the trail, all I could think was, "Ahh, I feel so much better." It was the freedom that I thought earthly truth would give me.

When you learn more of the truth and are living by it, you find yourself becoming a teacher. You have become available for Him to teach others that are put on your path. He can reach those people through you.

When that happens, you are His hands, His feet, His body, and He is inputting the truth in you through the Holy Spirit (the helper He said He would send), and it becomes a part of you. You find yourself saying things, talking about scripture and God's love to someone, and you think to yourself, "Did I just say that?" The words sound too profound to have come from you.

We are all born with intuition, the ability to hear and understand God's truth. That is what the Holy Spirit is, the small still voice you hear internally. We are never disconnected from God. All of us can use our intuition to connect to the Higher Heavens.

But you must get still, sit still in quiet. Be where you are. Do not sit in prayer asking God for things. Listen to what He says to you. He speaks to you, He really does. If you calm your mind, you will hear that still, calm, quiet voice inside you. That's your intuition, God's helper. It is the truth.

In our world, being calm and still is not easy to do. It is easier to numb yourself with things or people outside of yourself. It is easier to scroll through social media or have a few cocktails than to be calm and seek the truth. It is easier to spend an afternoon on Facebook than it is to deal with the pain inside you so that you can grow. There is nothing wrong with those things if they are used properly, but too often they are used to hide pain or to distract us from finding and living the truth.

Stop looking to external factors to find truth and happiness. Go within. Develop trust in God and learn how to listen to Him. That is the only true way to grow.

Over time, you will learn how to make better choices. If something feels good, like it is the right thing to do, then that is your guidance. That is the Holy Spirit talking to you. But if it feels wrong, then it is not the highest and best thing for you. It is not the truth, and it is not from God. If you start to do something out of self-will, and you feel sick in your stomach, but you think "I'll just ignore that," that is from Satan. Satan is poking you with his stick trying to move you to his team.

God's plan for my life and yours is cunning, baffling, and powerful. Our brains cannot comprehend God's plans for us. In the end, hopefully we will all end up with the source, with love, with God. It is your choice. He is that kind of Father to us, and He waits for you to choose Him.

Connecting

"I know the plans I have for you says the Lord...
to give you a future and a hope."
Jeremiah 29:11

That is one of my favorite Bible verses. I have it framed in my house. I read it each morning when I walk out my front door to go to work. It reminds me that I am not in control. And that is a good thing. God has already written the plan for my life. He was there at the beginning, and He will be there at the end. All I have to do is wake up, brush my teeth, have my quiet time with God, and walk out my front door. What happens each day is not up to me. God has it scripted out for me.

He weaves our lives like beautiful quilts. The underside of the quilt shows all the knots and open threads, but on top is a beautiful picture.

God weaved His plan for my life in such a subtle way that it has taken me until this moment for me to see the artistry of His hand. Nothing was wasted. Not one single experience. The pain, the abuse, the emotions, everything I had to endure along the way, were the path to my spiritual growth and how I reconnected with God. It took all of that trauma and disappointment for me to return home. I wish my journey had not required all of that. It was a lot of pain and devastation. But it was also part of His plan for me.

I previously shared that I sat on my bedroom floor begging God to please let me get so close to Him that I could lay my head on His lap and rest. Well, he granted my wish. I got what I wanted, but I had no idea of what it would take to get me there.

It does not matter what you call that still small voice within you. You could label it the zone, the force, something that passes all understanding. Whatever name you give it, it is God the Father, Christ Jesus the Son, and their Helper, the Holy Spirit.

If you choose to connect to God and enjoy a relationship with Him, you will have an internal therapist. You can connect to it in an instant. All you have to do is close your eyes and listen. You will feel the guidance in your inner knowing. It is incredibly quiet and amazingly simple.

Love yourself. You deserve it. God loves you beyond your understanding. I know it is hard to fathom, challenging to take in and comprehend.

Regardless of what anyone thinks or believes is possible, you can accomplish amazing things. They are already planned for you. Just step out. Put one foot in front of the other. Breathe, believe, and trust your angels.

The Apostle Paul calls us "living temples." When we have a genuine intimate relationship with God, we feel him living inside us. It is an honor. You wake up every day knowing that there is an active energy alive inside of you. It is a feeling, a knowing, a sensation that you know in your knower, as Pastor Harris used to say.

What you choose to call it isn't important. What is important is that you start to develop a relationship with your source energy, God and the Holy Spirit, that is not only surrounding you but is within you. This is the same energy that we came into Earth with, and it will be the best friend you have ever have if you open your heart, reach out your hand, and grab hold.

Here is the thing: Each and every one of us is connected to this limitless power. We are not using even a fourth of what this energy, this connection to the Holy Spirit, is waiting to give us.

When you foster a relationship with this amazing source of energy, when you commit to believing in the not yet seen but felt, you will stay in the highest frequency and harness your God-given power to create the reality that God had planned for you.

I am not boastfully telling you that this has been easy for me. It has taken me, at the writing of this book, more than thirty-four years. It has taken me more than three decades to research and delve into who I am. I have repeatedly asked, "Who is this woman? Why is she here? What does she stand for?"

I have tried to dissect who I am, like the layers of an onion. I have tried to reach the core and have an "aha" moment, where I know I have reached the truth and there are no more layers to find. I have been able to stand back and get a broader view of my life and see how it all fits together like a painting. I understand my existence, how I fit into this universe, and why God created me in the beginning.

Understanding, or wanting to understand, is not enough. You have to take action to find the truth and to live in the truth.

There is a place between action and reaction. In the expanse of that moment lies your power to choose a response, to stop at reason. If you close the door between body and soul and open the door between soul and spirit all will be good.

I hope the journey that God has planned for me will in some small way guide you to the light, the one and only light any of us has for eternity. Our forever Home. I am a vessel that God uses to bring more light to the world to the people who cross my path. I want God to be immensely proud of me when I get back home.

People like me who have crossed over have shared with me that God asks you a question when you return home. The question is, "What was your best thing?" Right here, right now, I can honestly say my best moment is, "Being the vessel to bring the spirit of my son into this world." The rest has been my education in Earth School that God planned for me from the beginning of my existence so that I could return home to be with Him as soon as possible.

What is your best thing? Each of us has that answer, that one special moment that made you know in the core of your very being, "This is what I was meant to be here for."

Why are you here?

Beginning, Ending, and Beginning Again

Here we are, at the end of my book. But is it really the end? It may be the end of the words printed on these pages, but it's not the end of my journey. And it shouldn't be the end of yours, either. Hopefully, you will take some lessons from my story, apply them to your life, and move closer to the person God wants you to be.

Life is not a drill or a test that has definite beginnings and endings. It is a series of seemingly unconnected events that span years and decades. It is a melody that will echo in your heart, and you will feel its energy, a sensation that lets you know that you are going where you were always supposed to be. As Mother Teresa said, "When you know how much God is in love with you then you can only live your life radiating that love."

Unfortunately, the journey is not always smooth. The people who come into our lives are often focused on putting up roadblocks that keep us from becoming the magnificent creatures that God meant us to be. It defies my imagination how cruel humans can be to each other.

I have survived to tell the story. My story. However difficult it is or will be, God has called me to tell it. If anyone reads this and my words help them get through their pain and grow from their own awareness, it has been worth it. It is the least I can do to answer God's calling for my life.

My scars are from all the times when life or the people in my life tried to knock me down. Those forces lost. I got back up every time. I am still standing. I am still moving forward. Some days, I move leaps and bounds, and my progress is clear. On other days, I move so slowly that it is hard to see if I have moved at all. And on other days, I move backwards and have to relearn lessons or tackle new ones.

I believe one of the worst things we can do is judge each other. We do not know each other's life stories. We have no way of comprehending each other's childhood trauma, their abuse, all of the events that shaped us into the people we became. We all have a past. That is part of God's plan for each one of us. The lessons we learned in the past, often the hard way, are His teaching tools.

One of the men I dated went behind my back and had one of his law enforcement buddies run a background check on me. That report pulled up every mistake I had made and every obstacle I had overcome. The man read that information and decided I was not worthy of his time or attention, and we stopped going out. What bothered me was that he only read the words on the paper and used them to judge me without talking to me or getting context. That decision cost us the possibility of what might have been a special relationship.

When we know that we all have a past, we remember to extend love and grace to each other. We respect how far we have come, how we have healed and grown into new people.

My past, every bad decision and every miserable relationship, was part of God's perfect plan for my life. He put all those experiences into my plan. He knew He would help me survive. It was the story that He gave me that I can share with all of you and help you move past the hurt in your life.

God loves us so much. He died on the cross so that we can come home to live with Him in eternity. While we are still here in Earth School, we can feel the love He has for us, and we can share our love with Him and the people around us.

As you go about your daily life, remember we are all learning. You are, I am, and every person you see and meet are in Earth School. The place, the destination we are all headed to, is the same. We are all going home to be with God.

As you face challenges and have to fight your way through tough times, think of me, of my heartbreak, my pain and suffering, and then remember all the wonderful and amazing healing and love God sent to me. That is the true gift of life.

When you make the choice to stand up and tell the truth, there is a lot you will be risking. Friends may leave you and your biological family might turn against you. If you were born into a toxic family as I was, there are rules about the family that you are supposed to adhere to. I broke one of those rules, and I have been punished for it.

But I would rather be me than them, as they live with the lies they have unconsciously promised to keep. Do I miss the family members who have thrown me out of their lives? More than I can describe. I experience daily pain from not having those family connections. But losing those ties was necessary for my survival, and I accept and understand why they could not be a part of my recovery. It was not their time. They were not ready.

One of my biggest challenges was to let God control my life. Most of the time, I think I've let go or feel like I have. Then it's dark, and I am alone. I want to engage, and in my mind, I go through my contact list searching for the people I will call. A voice comes into my mind and says, "No. I'm working on this. Quit! Stop! Let me do this for you." I come to my senses and tell myself to breathe, to believe, and to have faith.

This is not easy. I want to take back control all the time. Then my guardian angel reminds me of the times I have done that and the pain I chose to cause myself. It gives me the will to allow God to make choices for my life and complete the beautiful plan He has for me. Hope floods in, and I feel stress leave my physical body.

Being in control is not my job anymore. It never was. I imagined that I had control, but now realize I never did, and that is good news.

When you have painful experiences in your life it's natural to ask, "Why is this happening to me?" The answer is that God created you to have a human experience, and He knows the best way to help you grow through whatever difficulty touches you so that you can get back home to Him as soon as possible.

When I died and crossed over, the intense love I experienced was beyond anything earthly. It emanated around me. I could feel love engulf me and bring me in. God is not doing harmful things to any of us. Situations and experiences in our lives that seem painful and cruel are teaching tools.

God has set a path before me, and I am on it. I'm walking it one day at a time with my faith to give me strength to preserve as John did in the Bible. He continued. He pressed on. He preached. He shared his faith, his experience, and his hope in what he witnessed and saw in his relationship with Jesus. I can only hope that in some small way I can be close to that kind of witness for the love of Jesus.

I am attempting to share with all of you the truth, the truth as I have learned it throughout my life. My pastor, Nick Harris, asked me this question, and now I want to ask it to you: If your best friend handed you a beautifully wrapped gift for Christmas, what would you do? You would probably say, "Thank you so much for your amazing gift. I'm so grateful." You would never hand it back and say, "No, I don't want your gift. Thanks anyway."

If that is the case, when God gives you a beautifully wrapped gift with your name on it, why do you give it back?

Every day, God is handing you a huge gift that is wrapped with beautiful paper and a big bow. Accept the gift. Open it gladly, wrap yourself in it, and share it with the people around you. Your life will never be the same.